M000189855

PRAISE FOR *DANCING WITH DISRUPTION*

"Linda Rossetti has written an exposé and guide for anyone who has experienced disruption and displacement—in other words, for almost everyone these days. Her roadmap is accessible, insightful, artful, and intelligent. Reading it you will feel that she already knows you!" —**Dr. Roberta Herman**, president, Joslin Diabetes Center

"This book couldn't have come at a more perfect time. Linda Rossetti grants permission in the face of challenge to reflect on who we are and why we show up. A must-read for those looking for the courage to redefine themselves." —**Melanie Rosenwasser**, CPO, Dropbox

"Infused with hard-won wisdom, the world urgently needs the voice of Linda Rossetti in her brilliantly written new book. *Dancing with Disruption* illuminates and constructively guides us through the often-misunderstood disruptive and disorienting times in our lives. With her guiding steps, we can reframe our emotions; update the expectations we carry for ourselves; create a new self-concept; and connect with others. Most importantly, we can discover new expressions of who we are." —**Deb Guy**, executive director, Women's Exchange

"I have known Linda since her days at Harvard Business School where, then too, she approached the world with unbounded curiosity. It is no surprise to me that Linda has taken on this under-discussed yet nearly universal human experience and created such a powerful new toolkit. Her approach is an artful blend of solid research, deep understanding, and a palpable desire to help others to succeed. This is an across-the-board worthy read. "—**James I. Cash**, PhD, professor emeritus, Harvard Business School

"This book is a must-read for anyone experiencing a major life disruption or planning for a life transition. It offers a courageous perspective and stands apart thanks to Linda's wisdom, insights, and deeply moving stories." —**Lynn Perry Wooten**, president, Simmons University, and author, *Arrive and Thrive: 7 Impactful Practices for Women Navigating Leadership* and *The Prepared Leader: Emerge from Any Crisis More Resilient Than Before*

"In *Dancing with Disruption*, Linda turns her curiosity and powerful intellect to creating a model for positive change. An insightful, deeply meaningful work that offers us a roadmap for professional and personal success." —**Bob Brennan**, chair, BitSight, former CEO, Iron Mountain, and former CEO, Veracode

"A powerful blueprint for personal growth. In *Dancing with Disruption*, Linda Rossetti delivers a strategy and the tools to propel you forward. Adopt her mindset and anything is possible." —**Patricia Kolias**, triathlete, Ironman World Championship, Kona Qualifier

"My belief is that the obvious solution is not always the optimal solution. Linda offers us a courageous, insightful resource that empowers us to make different choices as we encounter personal and professional obstacles. I recommend this to anyone looking to meet uncertainty with confidence and courage!" —**Laura Huang**, international bestselling author, *Edge*, and professor, Harvard Business School

"I am inspired by the outstretched hand Linda extends through this thought-provoking, transformative approach. She offers us a fresh, courageous, and extensively researched perspective that is essential for anyone at the crossroads of their lives." —**Coco Brown**, founder and CEO, Athena Alliance

"Some disruptions are done to us and others by us—how we embrace them, learn from them, and self-discover in their wake is at the heart of this very important book for our time. A transformative read—one that ensures *all* take pride in their own voice, courage, and resilience." —**Deb Hicks**, leadership coach, former CPO, Dana Farber Cancer Institute

Dancing with Disruption

A New Approach to Navigating Life's Biggest Changes

Linda Rossetti

ROWMAN & LITTLEFIELD
Lanham • Boulder • New York • London

Published by Rowman & Littlefield
An imprint of The Rowman & Littlefield Publishing Group, Inc.
4501 Forbes Boulevard, Suite 200, Lanham, Maryland 20706
www.rowman.com

86-90 Paul Street, London EC2A 4NE

British Library Cataloguing in Publication Information Available

Library of Congress Cataloging-in-Publication Data
Names: Rossetti, Linda, author.
Title: Dancing with disruption : a new approach to navigating life's biggest changes / Linda Rossetti.
Description: Lanham, Maryland : Rowman & Littlefield Publishers, [2023] | Includes bibliographical references and index.
Identifiers: LCCN 2022042740 (print) | LCCN 2022042741 (ebook) | ISBN 9781538169377 (cloth) | ISBN 9781538169384 (ebook)
Subjects: LCSH: Self-actualization (Psychology) | Conduct of life.
Classification: LCC BF637.S4 R6749 2023 (print) | LCC BF637.S4 (ebook) | DDC 158.1—dc23/eng/20221212
LC record available at https://lccn.loc.gov/2022042740
LC ebook record available at https://lccn.loc.gov/2022042741

For my two stars, Jacqui and William

Contents

Illustrations

Illustrations by Maxwell Schwear

Acknowledgments

This book stands on the shoulders of the incredible people who participated in my research. While I would love to name each and every person, I committed to protecting their anonymity in exchange for their participation. For all those who contributed, thank you for your trust and your willingness to share so much of yourselves with me. Your courageous contributions shape every page of this book. *Thank you.*

Great thanks also to my readers who offered feedback throughout this book's evolution, including Robyn Bolton, Lina Gallotto, Seema Karunakaran, Steve Low, Stephen Malone, Vera Ng'oma, Jonathan Schlesinger, and Susan Price.

Thank you also to the incredible team that worked with me through the manuscript's development, including Sophie Wadsworth, Jeff Campbell, Benay Bubar, Maxwell Schwear, and Alicia Simons. I also want to thank Suzanne Staszak-Silva and John Willig for their belief in me and my ability to tell this story.

I also want to acknowledge the many people who served as my cheering squad and always made time for a phone call from me as I worked through this project, including Diane Cullen, Lisa deMont, Nancy Malone, Marla McDonald, Amy Orsenigo, Jeff Perrin, Amy Rutstein Riley, and Karen Williams. Thank you also to the entire staff at the Winchester, Massachusetts, Public Library.

Most of all, I would like to thank my children, Jacqui and William, for their incredible smiles and their unceasing belief in me.

Introduction

"It took a lot to come here today," says Janelle, a forty-one-year-old nurse who sits opposite me in a small conference room.

This morning, she and four others have joined me for coffee to talk about major changes in their lives. A digital tape recorder sits in the center of the table beside a tray of uneaten breakfast pastries.

"For the first time—I think ever—I am asking myself, *What do I want to do? Who do I want to be?*"

Janelle takes a breath, looks at the others around the table, and then adds in a near whisper, "I get this feeling that there is more for me."

The others smile and nod in encouragement.

"This is not easy. I've been going through the paces in my life, trying to not let my anxiety take over. I'm finding it harder and harder to show up."

She looks straight at me and says, "I am grateful for this conversation because no one else gets this. I have never felt so alone."

The others follow, in turn, with their own stories of upheaval.

As I listen, I hear commonalities in the way they tell their stories: in the emotions, like anxiety and disbelief, that take over, and in the impact that these experiences have on their sense of self. These patterns feel shared even though the group differs in age, profession, and circumstance. What is even more striking is that each of these capable people talks about their experience of upheaval as if they are the only ones to encounter it.

I keep wondering to myself as I sit there, *Why is no one talking about this?*

I mark that morning's conversation as a turning point in my life. From then on, I set out to understand times of upheaval in adult lives and, more importantly, how individuals, like Janelle, might respond.

This desire to understand drew me to hundreds of other individuals in conference rooms and coffee houses across the nation. Those who joined me brought me to their most important moments with stories of both pain and triumph.

The generosity of these strangers helped me learn an extraordinary amount about what is happening for Janelle and others like her, and shaped what I now know as a transformative opportunity available to all of us.

I credit these individuals with something else, too. The practice of hearing their stories felt like scaffolding to me at a time when I too felt buffeted by uncertainty. Thanks to their gift, I pay it forward here with their stories, and my own, about a problem that has no name.

UPHEAVAL AND PROMISE: WHY AM I TELLING THIS STORY?

Before we go on, I want to tell you why I was sitting with Janelle and the others that day. In many respects, I belonged on *their* side of the table. I had invited them to join me as part of my decision to take my blog, called Novofemina.com, to the next level. I started the blog to help me make sense of an unsettling time in my life.

This period occurred in my late forties when I found myself confused and alone in ways I had never experienced before. I felt unmoored in spite of working as a C-suite executive at a global Fortune 500 company, having two healthy young children, and enjoying a home in a town that was safe and welcoming for our family. There was nothing catastrophic that I could point to as a reason for my coming undone. I wondered, similar to what I heard from the others that morning, *What's wrong with me?*

I thank my lucky stars that I arrived that morning with Janelle having spent decades in the business world. There, I developed an expertise at solving poorly defined problems. My experience taught me that other people play a critical role in solving such mysteries. I knew sitting there that day that others could lead me to the answers I sought.

My business background inspired me to conduct research that ultimately included conversations with 270 other individuals. These people talked with me about a variety of changes they experienced in their lives. There were stories about family friction, job loss, career change, emotional turmoil, workforce re-entry, health challenges, coming out, the loss of a loved one, marriage, remarriage, divorce, a long-awaited promotion, childbirth, menopause, geographic moves between cities or countries, and more. Their stories, while threaded with emotions like fear, shame, and possibility, also pointed to a growing awareness of and questions about their sense of self.

While these stories were illuminating, I wanted a way to understand more about what I was hearing. I took a deep dive into scholarly research so that I could interpret more objectively what these people were saying. This step led me to extraordinary thinkers from the fields of neurology, psychology, psychiatry, human development, biology, Eastern religions, and leadership. This book stands on the shoulders of these brilliant thinkers.

These early steps acted like wind in my sails. I wrote my first book, *Women and Transition: Reinventing Work and Life*, and began speaking and conducting seminars based upon my initial research. These activities led me to launch a podcast, *Destination Unknown: A Field Guide*, to open up a conversation about how shifts in our sense of self express themselves in our lives. I then initiated more research in collaboration with local university professors. Through it all, I connected with more individuals for whom *upheaval*—especially during the pandemic—and *promise* showed up together amidst the circumstances of their lives.

Dancing with Disruption is an invitation to change how you respond to shifts in your thinking about who you are. It will transform your understanding of what is occurring at such times and guide you through a step-by-step toolkit that can empower you to become your fullest self. This understanding and toolkit will build your confidence such that you can make different choices in the face of uncertainty:

choices not motivated by fear or constraints, but instead buoyed by optimism, excitement, and with the courage to reach for what previously felt unimaginable.

If you hold fast to your sense of possibility, and we embark on this journey together, *Dancing with Disruption* can help you positively alter the trajectory of your life.

WHY DOES THIS BOOK MATTER NOW?

This work feels even more urgent now than when I sat down with Janelle a decade ago thanks to a perfect storm of factors.

Structural changes in the workplace and sharply reduced employee tenure are translating into the need for more and more of us to reimagine our identity as it relates to our occupation. This dynamic is due, in part, to the fact that technology has begun to deliver its long-promised efficiencies, from the use of robotics on the manufacturing floor, to software that tracks every move of remote workers, to an ability to close a business's accounting books with the click of a button. These advances reduce the number and type of jobs available, putting pressure on an individual's need to reimagine their self-concept as it relates to employment.

A growing list of positive social gains, like advances in longevity and the embrace of the gender continuum, invite adults to reinvent their self-concept repeatedly during adulthood.

And, finally, the pandemic's powerful imprint has increased the willingness of many of us to redefine the underlying assumptions upon which our self-concept is anchored. We are quitting jobs and changing careers, moving to new locations, and questioning *why* this all matters.

My research underscores these trends and points to a new era in identity renewal, one in which shifts in our sense of self will be normalized.

Let's face it. This notion of exploring shifts in our thinking about who we are—our identity—is countercultural. As a society, we love sticky identities. We are physicians or firefighters or professional athletes or great neighbors. We often greet those who entertain such shifts cruelly; they are excluded, mocked, or treated as if there were something wrong with their constitution or character.

I remember when I explained my own feeling of being unmoored to my mother. She said, "Oh, it is just your midlife crisis."

After a decade of research on the topic, I can confidently tell her and others, "No, this has nothing to do with age, nor is it a crisis." Shifts in our thinking about our self-concept are a normal part of adult life and signal an invitation for transformational growth that can have a lasting positive effect on our lives.

HOW CAN THIS BOOK HELP?

This book explores four kinds of circumstances common at times of major change in life which may address your particular situation.

The first situation involves the experience of unplanned events, like a job loss or a divorce. Many who experience such changes toggle back and forth between a desire to get "back" to normal and a willingness to embrace new thinking.

Others find themselves feeling stuck or frustrated at their inability to make progress in addressing a desired change. Individuals in this category have historically navigated major changes with some success and now wonder, *Why is this one any different?*

Another set of circumstances arises for those who anticipate a major change and are interested in understanding how best to prepare. The people I meet in this category are often readying for a milestone-related passage, like graduation, retirement, or a significant birthday.

Finally, there are those who want to be proactive in addressing a realization of some kind, like a feeling that something is not right or a desire to pursue more of their potential.

Dancing with Disruption is designed to help you greet uncertainty related to major changes in your life differently and empower you to move forward with confidence in the direction of your dreams.

WHAT WILL YOU DISCOVER?

Dancing with Disruption moves through a series of real-life vignettes, my own and those taken from my research conversations. These stories are excerpted from hundreds of hours of taped discussions. They are de-identified such that I can deliver on my commitment to maintain the privacy of all those who participated. Even though I cannot name them personally, I am forever indebted to them for their willingness to share so much of themselves with me. Together, we created an invaluable chronicle of transformative journeys in adult lives.

The book is told in three parts. Part I introduces you to a new vocabulary for and increases your understanding of what is happening at periods of major change in your life. It debunks common myths and addresses a long-held assumption that equates personal upheaval with the need for a departure, like leaving a relationship or a job. Part I enables you to think differently about these times and empowers you to make new choices, choices not driven by fear or constraints, but choices instead rooted in a confidence to pursue the dreams you hold only in your heart.

Part II addresses the resistance you meet when you attempt to make changes in your life, particularly emotional resistance—like anger, guilt, and regret. This section also introduces the Incubator, a step-by-step toolkit that is designed to support your transformative journey. Two concepts play a critical role in this section: the *choices* you make, and your awareness of and willingness to lead with your *voice*. Voice, for our purposes, refers to your essence, your own truth.

Finally, Part III introduces the Incubator's individual tools and walks you through your own step-by-step transformative process. You will learn how to move forward regardless of the opposition you meet and the enormity of your dreams. This systematic approach involves four tools, including those that help you reimagine your self-concept and redefine the narrative you use in talking with others while you are "in between." The Incubator is flexible; you can use its tools sequentially or in an order that makes sense for you. This design ensures that you make real progress on living into the fullness of who you are.

In many ways, this book is designed as a workbook. Throughout it, you are invited to complete two types of journaling prompts: Reflections and Check Steps. Each chapter features a Reflection that helps you translate the chapter's ideas into your own experience. The Incubator's chapters (Chapters 6 through 9) invite you to complete an additional journaling prompt, a Check Step. These Check Steps help you create and refine your own transformative plan for moving forward. Trina, a forty-three-year-old mother and solopreneur who worked with the Incubator after a divorce and a crushing mid-career setback, said, "This process has touched my life tremendously. The work gave me the courage to overcome my fears and take the plunge into a new and exciting world."

Dancing with Disruption will deepen your understanding of and the skills necessary for responding differently to times of upheaval in your life. It is an invitation to choose something unique and irreplaceable at such moments, a fuller expression of *you*.

A NOTE BEFORE YOU BEGIN

This book and the research that stands behind it are nothing short of a labor of love. I hope it helps you transform what could be a terrifying and unsettling period in your life into one of promise and great joy. In many ways, this is the book I wish I had found when I was in a place similar to the one Janelle described that morning in the conference room. The process you will learn about in the upcoming pages is intended to help you bring fresh thinking to moments of upheaval in your life and empower you to respond differently by relying on newfound confidence to make choices that can positively impact your life.

In the end, I hope that this book helps you come to know, trust, and turn up the volume on your own voice. I have come to know that shifts in your sense of self are signaling an opportunity to rely on your own voice more fully. As you will learn, I was fooled by this connection to voice. For decades, I wholeheartedly believed I was listening to my own voice. Yet, the techniques you will learn in the upcoming pages revealed gaps in my voice's strength and my connection to it. That awareness, and my attempt to address the gaps, have changed my life in ways I never anticipated when I first sat down to talk with Janelle and the others.

In many respects, I started this book that day. I am eternally grateful to those first individuals and the many others who stepped forward to share their experiences with me. They also gave me new insight into the impact of our collective voices. I always knew that our voices were, and

still are, critical. Yet, in listening to those in my research, I now understand on a deeper level how individual voices play the first and most
critical part in broader change. As a lifetime advocate for equity, I can
tell you that the book itself will not eliminate the injustices that I and
others work hard to address in our world. What it can do is strengthen
your voice, a necessary precursor to improving our lives as well as the
policies and institutions that affect us all.

   Dancing with Disruption is an invitation to the journey of a lifetime.
I am profoundly grateful for the gifts this process brought into my
life. I hope the same will be true for you. Thank you for giving me the
opportunity to share its incredible promise with you.

                                                        Linda Rossetti

I

UNDERSTANDING DISRUPTION

1

An Unlikely Invitation

"I don't know which way to turn," says Melanie, a single, forty-one-year-old equity analyst who met me for coffee at a small indie coffee shop near her apartment in Cambridge, Massachusetts. "I never imagined that I would be without work at this point in my life." As she speaks, she tilts her head sideways as if struggling to make sense of her own words. "That I am even saying this to you is making me anxious."

A mutual friend put Melanie in touch with me. My friend made the introduction because she knew of my research on major changes in adult lives. Thanks to that work, Melanie's words, while heartbreaking, were very familiar to me.

Melanie holds two degrees, one in math and the other in international finance. She spent eight years working in Hong Kong's financial services industry. "I do not define myself by my work, but my job and what I have accomplished are a big part of who I am."

"I am scared," she continues, melting away a practiced veneer of calm. "I don't know what to do."

Melanie left Hong Kong to join a finance start-up in New York. "Things at the bank in Hong Kong had not gone as well as I had hoped. I jumped at the chance to move back to the States," she says. New York represented a fresh start for her. I could hear it in her voice.

"I was so excited! The company was really cool. We were working on a new online-trading algorithm."

In recalling her start in New York, she says, "Early meetings with my new boss did not go as I planned. I guess I asked too many questions. Honestly, I could not believe what was happening. He made decisions that were damaging to the group." She shakes her head as if she cannot believe what she is saying. "When he screwed things up, he got more responsibility!"

When the start-up company's next round of financing was delayed, staffing cuts came. Melanie was not the least bit surprised when she was asked one day to walk down the corridor to the company's large conference room. There, she learned that her position was being eliminated.

In the twenty months since that ill-fated meeting, Melanie doggedly looked for a new role in "fintech"—a term for the financial technology industry supporting equity analysts like her.

"I've been out so long," she says with a sigh of resignation. "There must be something wrong with me! I cannot seem to focus," she adds, bewilderedly. Try as she might, she feels disconnected from her detail-oriented persona. In a tone of resignation, she adds, "I am such a failure."

Do you define yourself primarily with one endeavor, like Melanie? What might happen if you experienced a break in your connection to it?

On this question, Melanie is clear. "This is affecting my *whole life*," she says. "Everything I thought was the right thing to do is not working."

She muses, "I am an equity analyst. I am not sure if I want any part of that world anymore."

At first glance, Melanie's story may appear steeped in particulars that position her experience as a uniquely individual one. Our work together will persuade you that her experience is worthy of a second look because what makes her experience disruptive might not be what immediately comes to mind.

WHAT IS A DISRUPTION?

A disruption, for our purposes, is a break or interruption in our personal experience. Disruptions come in all shapes and sizes, from a flat tire on the way to work to a radically new way of being after getting remarried and combining two families into one household. They can involve events, like a divorce or a relocation; feelings, like boredom or rage; and circumstances, like coming of age.

By our definition, Melanie experienced a host of disruptions over the many months she described during our conversation, including her job loss, two geographic moves—one from Hong Kong to New York and a second from New York to Cambridge—feeling defeated after a prolonged absence from the workforce, being rejected many times as a candidate for a new job, feeling like a failure, spending too much time alone, and feeling optimistic after she was moved to the final round of an interview process. Any of these and countless other events, circumstances, and feelings could have been disruptive for Melanie.

Melanie's experience put her in good company with the more than two hundred adults who shared their stories of major life changes with me through my research. There was Thomas, a single biotech salesperson who struggled to make sense of what to do with himself after an unanticipated job loss coincided with the breakup and departure of his longtime significant other. Or Arushi, whose world felt chaotic and out of control after her husband's job loss created an urgent need for her to return to the workforce after a fifteen-year absence. Or Irene, a mid-forties mom of twins who was overjoyed to be getting remarried. Or Maureen, whose beliefs about herself, marriage, and family were upended when her spouse announced he was leaving her to be with another man. Or Tiffany, who set out to reignite the passion she once held for work after years of boredom. Or Jason, a husband and father who grieved for a part of himself that was missing after his wife and the mother of their twenty-four-month-old daughter lost her battle with pancreatic cancer.

While all of these people experienced disruption in many forms, I hope to convince you that there are similar threads to their experiences that are too often overlooked or ignored. Sadly, I might add. These common patterns offer valuable insights and help us reposition disruption, which can be a disorienting and emotionally charged experience, as having the potential to serve as a gateway for extraordinary possibilities in our lives.

I want to take a moment to acknowledge our experience of disruption. We are socialized to *act* in the face of disruption, a bias that can take many forms, like repairing, moving beyond, or taking immediate action. In this vein, we "do, do, do, and then do some more." Thanks to this, we turn quickly to thinking about "what to do" when faced with a disruption. While honoring this bias for action, I want to slow down our thinking about disruption by first talking through our experience of it, separate and apart from our response to it. Our work in this chapter will focus entirely on our experience of disruption. We will leave our response to disruption for Chapter 2.

I find it most useful to think about our experience of disruption along two dimensions: its *impact* on how we function, and its *influence* on our thinking about who we are.

THE LENS OF IMPACT

Impact refers to how we function in the wake of a disruption. I like to think about such an impact along a continuum (Figure 1.1). At one end of the spectrum, a disruption's impact on how we function is minimal. Here we effortlessly re-establish our familiar routine. For example, a traffic jam on the way to work may be disruptive, but our ability to be back to "normal" in its wake is nearly effortless. We may be late for work and truly frazzled by the time we arrive there, but by lunchtime, the occurrence is nearly forgotten.

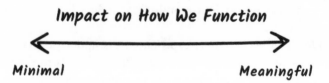

Figure 1.1.   Impact on How We Function.

I put the word "normal" in quotations in the previous paragraph because everyone has their own level of functioning. A single dad with four school-aged children has one level of normal functioning, while my neighbor, who is disabled and uses a wheelchair, has an entirely different normal level of functioning. The continuum speaks to your own familiar routine.

At the opposite end of the spectrum, a disruption may impact our functioning more significantly. In Melanie's case, she reported that she was less able to prepare as usual for upcoming interviews, even though she was characteristically a detail-oriented person. Try as she might, she could not re-establish her typical routine. This disruption led to a meaningful impact on her functioning.

THE LENS OF INFLUENCE

Melanie's experience also illustrates the other important dimension of our lived experience of disruption: its influence on our thinking about who we are.

Like impact, a disruption's influence on our thinking about our sense of self differs widely (Figure 1.2). On the far left, a disruption's influence on our sense of self is extremely low. Like the person who encountered a traffic jam on the way to work, the interruption had virtually no influence on her self-concept.

At the other end of the continuum, we can experience a high degree of influence on our thinking about who we are. Here Melanie questioned her connection to an identity as an equity analyst, which had been the unifying structure for her self-concept for her entire adult life.

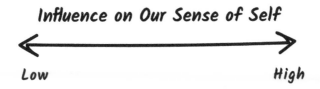

Figure 1.2. Influence on Our Sense of Self.

A CASE STUDY ON DISRUPTION

Seema, a dynamic thirty-year-old living in San Francisco, was well aware of the impact and influence of disruption in her world. While unanticipated, Seema gained an important lens into her sense of self through the experience.

"It all started when I said to myself, *What am I doing? I don't believe in this anymore*," Seema shares with me. Her realization was shocking and unexpected.

It all began with a phone call from her mother that Seema received while she was at work. As soon as she heard her mother's tone, she knew it would be best to find a place with some privacy to take the call. She stepped outside to continue the conversation.

"'I have breast cancer' are the only words I could make out above my mother's crying and screaming," Seema says, explaining how she herself crumbled at the word "cancer."

Many of us have been on the receiving end of such a call and had to carry the weight of a word like "cancer" or another significant crisis. We all process it differently. In Seema's case, it opened her up to deep questions about her identity.

For as long as Seema could remember, she was achievement oriented. She joined a prestigious West Coast investment bank after graduating from Georgetown University with a degree in finance. "My whole life, from high school on, I have always been very busy and very, very focused," she offers as she quickly ticks off accolades she received along the way: high honors throughout school, three varsity high school sports, and Division I college basketball.

"I knew exactly what was in front of me at every turn," she says, leaning toward me. "Once I started in investment banking, I knew that in three years I would be a manager, and then in four more years, I would be a managing director. My focus was always to strive for the next rung." Seema was two years into her banking job when she received that pivotal phone call from her mother.

"I was working easily seventy-five hours a week at the time," she explains. Seema slotted work meetings around her mom's chemo infusions, made food for her parents in the wee hours of the morning, and dropped meals off at her parents' apartment on her way to work every day. Still, it was not as much as she wanted to do. "Knowing that I couldn't be there more for my mother was really kind of draining me at a time when, of course, she needed me."

"My mother was not doing very well," she continues. "The doctors kept adjusting her medications. It hit her really hard. She kept talking about not wanting to wake up in the morning." Alarmed, Seema and her family arranged to attend a special counseling session one evening. "We wanted to know how to help my sick mother. I needed to be there by 7 p.m.

"I lied to my colleagues that one night. I do not even remember what excuse I gave them. My colleagues and I would work until eight or ten every night. The punch line is that I did not feel comfortable telling them I was going to a family counseling session.

"It was at that point that I really thought, *Why am I in this rat race at the firm, trying to get to the next deadline or make the next buck for our partners?* Feeling like I had to lie to be with my family . . . that was the tipping point for me."

Sitting across from Seema, I can tell how difficult that realization and her mother's illness had been for her. Until that point in her life, she had followed such a carefully curated path.

I ask Seema to describe how it felt to question her identity. "I think I was most surprised at how scared I was to even envision something else for me because of my traditional way of being," she says. "I had no idea what the right move was. I have always been a very calculated, focused person. I've always set a goal, known what I was going to do, and been able to execute it, whether academically, professionally, socially, or whatever."

Her sense of self wobbled under this conflict. "My belief at the time was simple," she explains. "I failed."

In spite of this harsh self-criticism, Seema did not back away from her realization. She knew she needed to get some temporary relief from the investment bank while she figured out what to do next. She looked for other work and quickly landed a temporary position in finance for a small company. Even amidst this success, *what was next* was terrifying. For the first time ever, her future was a blank slate.

I ask Seema to describe her experience of operating in such an uncertain place. She replies, "I felt like I was smothering; I had a recurring sense of anxiety, fear, and self-doubt. It was so scary knowing that I was no longer just executing, making the 'right' decisions, and moving on a forward path."

Our conversation winds the clock forward to where her courageous choice led nearly two years after her mom's initial phone call. "I joined a start-up here [in the Bay Area] in an operational role. It's so fun. It's amazing. And my mom is doing well," she says with a smile. "I never knew how happy this could make me. Like, I am so happy I did what I did. I would never have gotten the job I've got right now without making the scariest transition." She pauses and adds, "So many people told me I was crazy. It's so funny to think about that because this was really the best decision I ever made. It completely opened me up. I am so thankful. While I would never wish my mother's illness on anyone, I am thankful because it made me reflect on things I do not think I ever would have considered. It went against everything that I knew in terms of going for the safest, most practical solution." She thought a moment and finished with a broad, confident smile, "This path helped me get to know who I am as a person. I am not scared anymore."

While it can feel dangerous and countercultural to reach beyond the stability of our familiar self, we will learn that in doing so, we begin a process of discovery that offers unparalleled opportunities to all those who embark on such a journey.

WHEN OUR SENSE OF SELF FALTERS

Our experience of disruption at the far right of both continuums, like Seema's, can leave us in unchartered territory. Beth Anne, a forty-one-year-old mother of four children, experienced a substantial break in her thinking about who she was when she decided to leave her marriage.

Beth Anne and her husband were high school sweethearts and married after their respective college graduations. She landed a job right away as a kindergarten teacher in a small affluent community outside of Cincinnati. She left teaching when their second daughter was six months old.

Beth Anne's relationship with her husband was far from what she had imagined, but she never seriously considered divorce. "He would say things like, 'You don't make enough money,' or 'You're not pretty enough,' or 'You know you're not interesting,'" Beth Anne says. "I mean, just really horrible things." Even though she recognized her growing dissatisfaction with the marriage, she increased her resolve to make things work.

One day, she and her husband were scheduled to take their youngest child to a medical appointment with a specialist. They had waited weeks for the appointment. The punch line of the story is that her husband never showed up for the appointment as had been the plan.

"I knew right then in the doctor's office—it was over," Beth Anne recalls defiantly. That moment marked a turning point. Beth Anne became acutely aware of a gap between the expectations she held for herself and her experience in her marriage. She filed for divorce.

"I never wanted to be divorced. I never wanted to go down that path. I tried to save the marriage. Then I realized, it is ridiculous trying to save the marriage. The marriage could not be saved." Beth Anne pauses and adds, "It was painful and unwelcome."

Beth Anne's decision initiated an important shift. "Leaving the marriage came with letting go of everything I grew up with as far as values and what marriage meant. I was a wife and mother. The divorce led to a complete shift in my values."

A HIGHLY INDIVIDUAL EXPERIENCE

I want to take a moment to underscore that while disruption is a universal experience, how we individually experience it differs. While one person, like Beth Anne, may experience disruption as devastating and unwelcoming, another may experience it as valuable and advantageous. There is no *one way* or *right way* to experience disruption.

In the pandemic's early days, I spoke with two managers at Macy's corporate headquarters, both of whom had lost their jobs in the aftermath of the company's bankruptcy filing. They had dramatically different experiences.

One was disappointed by, and even angry about, the job loss but quickly went about replacing her income with little or no impact on her functioning or on her thinking about who she was. The other had the opposite experience. He struggled to make sense of the loss and the subsequent unraveling of his identity after his decades-long service to Macy's. That job and his connection to it were simply who he was. He felt rudderless, particularly in light of the additional financial, social, and well-being pressures brought on by the pandemic.

While disruption is universal, our experience of it will differ. At any age, whether we are twenty-two, fifty-two, or seventy-two years old, our experience of disruption is highly individual. There is no guarantee, as we saw in the Macy's example, that our experience of disruption will mirror another person's even though they may encounter an event or circumstance similar to our own. Our experience of disruption is a highly individual occurrence.

MEETING AT THE CROSSROADS

My research revealed an unmistakable pattern in our experience of disruption. Those individuals who experience disruptions with greater *impact* and/or *influence*, as shown in the illustrations, gain access to an unparalleled opportunity in their lives. We will refer to instances of these types of disruptions as "gateway disruptions." While this often runs counter to societal beliefs, gateway disruptions invite us to access enlivening new expressions of who we are.

Society teaches us to judge ourselves harshly when we experience a gateway disruption. For example, we are taught to ignore, tamp down, run the other way, or initiate innumerable distractions at the first sign of any wavering related to our self-concept. Those who entertain such shifts—shifts in thinking about who we are—are frequently disgraced, shamed, excluded, or questioned about potential problems in their constitution or character. These social norms lead us to grossly misinterpret these experiences and put at risk our ability to access the value they represent in our lives.

Gateway disruptions serve as an invitation to access unlimited possibilities in ourselves. Our work together will focus on creating a new vocabulary and understanding of what is occurring when we experience a gateway disruption, and introducing us to a toolkit that enables us to envision and realize our dreams.

◈

A REFLECTION: DISRUPTION AND YOU

Have you ever encountered a gateway disruption? To help you answer this question, we will now turn to our first Reflection. This book's Reflections are a series of question prompts designed to help you link the book's topics to your own experience. Each one is followed by a "Reflection-in-Action," which offers an example from those in my research who helped me test these activities.

I have my fingers crossed that you take the time to do each Reflection. I know it can be tempting to skip sections such as these; I have often done this as a reader myself, believing that I will go back and complete them later. If you invest the time, you will gain new ways of thinking about yourself and benefit from added momentum throughout your journey.

Before you start, please take a moment to create a place to store your responses to the Reflections that will allow you to refer back to them periodically. I recommend that you choose a format that works best for you; some use a journal or notebook, and others start a digital folder. Regardless of the format, these Reflections will bring your exploration to life.

Step 1: Have you ever experienced a gateway disruption? Write down any that come to mind.

> *Note, a gateway disruption is an experience that impacts how we function and/or influences how we think about who we are. Gateway disruptions can be initiated by events, feelings, or circumstances.*

Step 2: How did it feel to experience such a disruption?

> *For example, if you listed a geographic move, it might feel scary, exhausting, stressful, and/or exciting.*

Step 3: What might this experience of a gateway disruption mean for you?

For example, your geographic move might mean "a new start" after the breakup of a long-term relationship. It might also be something you have wanted to do for a long time.

REFLECTION-IN-ACTION

Sam, a fifty-four-year-old bioengineer, found this Reflection useful because it helped him bring a new perspective to his experience and ask himself questions that he felt were long overdue. Sam opted to take early retirement when his employer announced a restructuring that offered long-tenured employees a chance to participate in a lucrative early retirement program.

"I felt like I hit the lottery," Sam tells me. He planned to put the proceeds from the early retirement package in the bank and rejoin the workforce without interruption.

Things did not go as he had originally planned. "I've been out of work now for the better part of a year," he explains. His prolonged absence proved disruptive. Sam had an unexpectedly challenging time navigating unemployment and securing a new job.

"Honestly, my self-confidence has taken a big hit. You know, I get rejection and all, but looking for new work and not getting any positive response drains me badly." He takes a breath and continues: "I am fighting off measuring myself—negatively—against peers every day. But on the other side, I think I can do such-and-such a thing. I can run for office. I can be governor. Everything starts bubbling up again. Things I have not thought about in years.

"I made the decision about who I am—that has influenced every decision since—when I was eighteen," recalls Sam in a flabbergasted tone. "I chose bioengineering at eighteen and got married at twenty-one. *What did I know?*" His voice rises a few octaves on those last words. "Would you ask *an eighteen-year-old* for advice?" he asks me flatly with great concern.

Sam's disruption raised his awareness of questions about his self-concept that he had not considered for a very long time. "I am going to run this to ground," finishes Sam. "Not sure where it will lead. I am open to what might be next."

◆

CAUGHT IN MISCUES

Prior to conducting my research, I had my own significant experience with gateway disruptions. I not only disregarded the cues but also experienced increasingly concerning consequences thanks to my ignoring them.

Over a thirty-six-month period, I experienced a continuous stream of major disruptions. I welcomed two children, my dad passed away after a multi-year battle with cancer, and I sold the company I started and had continued to run. Any one of these experiences could have demanded my full attention and deposited me on the far right of the impact and influence continuums. What did I do in light of all this? I got a new job, put my head down, and kept going.

One day I unwittingly "borrowed" a stranger's car on the way home from work. Before we go into the details, let me tell you about the identity I had crafted for myself that put me in that situation in the first place.

I came of age in the 1980s with an undergraduate degree from an all-women's college and an MBA from the Harvard Business School. I was executive vice president for human resources and administration at Iron Mountain, a $3.5-billion-dollar Fortune 500 company, reporting to the company's CEO. My job carried responsibility for twenty-one thousand people in thirty-seven countries around the world. I had gotten that job by way of being the CEO of another company, a venture-capital-backed technology company that was acquired by a publicly traded corporation.

I do not share that background to impress you. I offer it to underscore the fact that I had labored my entire life to create that identity. It never crossed my mind to alter it or that it could shift in any fashion. Had I understood disruption, my experience of this drama and its aftermath would have been markedly different.

Here is my memory of how it unfolded.

This one day, my babysitter needs to leave at 5:30 p.m. on the dot, so I need to leave the office even earlier, a rarity. I run for the elevator at

4:59 p.m. When the elevator doors open three levels below ground, the two cars facing me are coincidentally the two cars owned by my household, a black Honda Pilot and a black Volvo Cross Country. I should mention that the garage required employees to leave the keys in our cars so that the attendants could move the cars as required throughout the day.

I hop in the Honda Pilot, put my phone in the center console, and begin my winding journey up three levels. At the garage's exit, I open the driver's side window, wave my badge in front of the electronic reader, and maneuver out onto the busy one-way street.

As the car clears the hulking building, the radio turns on to an unfamiliar station. I look around and realize for the first time that I am surrounded by a beige interior, not my car's smoky gray. *OMG. I am in the wrong car!*

By the time my brain catches up with what is happening, I am well away from the building, in thick traffic, hyperventilating.

Right turn, right turn, right turn. I circumnavigate the city block, open the window, swipe my badge, and re-enter the garage. "Are you stealing cars?" yells Joaquin, the lead attendant, whom I have known for years. He and his co-workers are laughing, thinking this is nothing short of hilarious. I do not stop. Round and round I go, down three levels.

I breathe for what feels like the first time in minutes when I see *my* car. I quickly park, grab my briefcase, and begin this all again.

For a second time, I drive the winding route up to the exit. The attendants are still laughing as I wave to them and say nothing more. I swipe my badge at the automatic reader and am out on the street. No radio. All good.

I turn to get my phone to call the babysitter. Only then do I realize my crushing error: I left my phone in the center console of the other vehicle!

Right turn, right turn, right turn. I circumnavigate the city block for a second time. I swipe my badge to re-enter the garage. The attendants now call out, "Are you going to take another car?" I half smile at them—as I have no time for details—and turn to head down three levels.

The other car is there, *thankfully.* I pull up, hesitate for a moment before I open the driver's side door, and lunge my upper body into the car to grab my phone.

Three levels up, the attendants are teary from laughter, as I later learn that they watched my phone drama on the guard booth's closed-circuit television. Out on the street, I auto-dial the babysitter, for whom I am now more than thirty minutes late. She is livid. I get it, completely.

What is wrong with me? I ask myself with deepening concern as I sit gridlocked in rush-hour traffic.

In the aftermath of this incident, I felt isolated, even more depleted, and unable to get my bearings. I could not put my finger on exactly what was happening outside of being aware that I was unraveling in uncharacteristic ways. Time-pressed, like many of us, I chalked up "borrowing a car" to a really bad day and kept going.

In hindsight, I can see that my unraveling at the garage was one of a string of increasingly severe signals. It seems as if they were all acting in unison to get my attention. I was unable to respond in any meaningful way because I lacked the equivalent of a disruption Rosetta Stone, the famous tablet that allowed researchers to interpret Egyptian hieroglyphics.[1] Our work in this book will serve in this capacity. It will allow us to interpret what is happening when we experience a gateway disruption and, importantly, how to realize the extraordinary value these occurrences represent in our lives.

YOUR INVITATION

Disruption is a common, frequently overlooked, deeply misunderstood occurrence that can serve as an on-ramp to realizing the dreams we hold only in our hearts. Gateway disruptions occur when an event, feeling, or circumstance meaningfully influences our thinking about who we are or impacts our ability to function. These gateway disruptions are common. They are not only for the five-time Olympic gold medalist who decides to leave her sport after an incredible run on the world's stage. Everyone encounters gateway disruptions at one time or another, including those who cling to outward appearances of success.

Dancing with Disruption introduces new thinking about what is happening when we encounter a gateway disruption and teaches us how to respond differently at these important times in our lives.

In this book, we will:

- Create a new understanding of gateway disruptions
- Explore the options available in response to such a disruption and what these choices mean
- Learn new techniques to skillfully navigate our chosen response
- Discover how to identify opportunities, pursue dreams that felt previously impossible, and ultimately live the lives we imagine

This book will position disruption as a platform for renewing our self-concept, a journey that can enable joyful, expansive, and enlivening growth. As we move forward in this journey together, you will learn how to embrace these invitations and make choices that can positively influence the trajectory of your life.

2

Responding to Disruption

How will you respond to disruption? The question seems straightforward, particularly when our experience of disruption involves very little impact on our ability to function and little to no influence on our self-concept. What about a gateway disruption? How will you respond in the wake of such an occurrence?

I know that *choosing* how to respond can feel inaccurate when we are in the throes of a disorienting and potentially heartbreaking disruption. For example, Aleen, a recently widowed fifty-nine-year-old, asks, "What choice do I have? My spouse died."

Aleen and her spouse had been preparing to celebrate their thirty-fifth wedding anniversary. "He collapsed one evening when he got up from his favorite chair to walk the dog," she says as her voice quivers. I reach out and take her hand. We stand there silently for a long moment, appreciating all that had passed in her world as of late. The support I offer does little to assuage her concern. Where is choice in her world of loss?

In this chapter, we will address Aleen's question by focusing on the choices available to us in response to a gateway disruption. We will explore the difference between two common responses: *change* and *transition*. And we will take the time to think through our own relationship with making choices. Together, we will learn that gateway disruptions do not prescribe a specific response, regardless of the circumstances surrounding them. Instead, they bring us to a powerful opportunity to choose our response in ways consistent with what holds value and meaning to us.

UNDERSTANDING CHANGE AND TRANSITION

At moments of disruption like Aleen's husband's death, we can respond in a variety of ways. We can cling to the status quo, we can hold fast to a place of imagined stability, we can change, or we can transition. While this range is oversimplified for our purposes, it features two common terms, "change" and "transition," that represent very different responses in the face of disruption.

We opt for *change* when we maintain a known expression of who we are, whereas we reach for *transition* when we are willing to explore shifts in our sense of self (Figure 2.1).

With change, we alter or vary particulars, like a hairstyle or an apartment, while we cling to stability in our self-concept. Changes involve a known outcome. When we choose change, we alter particulars to address the uncertainty surrounding the disruptive break. Change, as a response, leaves intact our beliefs about who we are.

With *transition*, we entertain shifts in thinking about our sense of self, a choice that welcomes instability for a time. In choosing transition, we re-examine the assumptions upon which our self-concept relies. Transition, as opposed to change, involves unknown outcomes. It serves as a platform for discovery through which we re-examine the assumptions we carry about who we are and how we make meaning in the world. The choice of transition in response to disruption represents our willingness to entertain an evolution in our thinking about who we are. With this response, we reimagine or transform our sense of self and open ourselves up to new—albeit unknown at our journey's outset—expressions of our identity. The choice of transition enables personal growth and new ways of seeing value in ourselves and in the world.

I find it helpful to think about the difference between change and transition as similar to hiking on a craggy mountain. On this mountain, the horizontal trails that encircle the mountain gain no elevation.

> ### Change & Transition through the Lens of Disruption
>
> ---
>
> *Change is a process through which we alter particulars and leave intact our assumptions upon which our sense of self relies.*
>
> *Transition is a process through which we re-examine our assumptions upon which we architect our sense of self.*

Figure 2.1.   Change and Transition through the Lens of Disruption

Each of these trails has only one spot that serves as a trailhead for a vertical ascent. Disruption deposits us at the ascent trailhead, which is a little overgrown but visible.

With change, we opt for another go-around on our horizontal loop. Keep in mind, go-arounds on the horizontal loops can feel like new paths because conditions on the mountain may have shifted since our last time around. As such, the same horizontal path may prove to be even more challenging than in the past. With transition, we chop through the overgrowth and head up the ascent trail to a higher horizontal trail on the mountain.

Change and transition represent two different choices in the face of disruption, each with its own relationship to our self-concept.

TWO RESPONSES

Arthur, similar to many others in my research, tells me a story of both change *and* transition. "A great gift has been given to me," he starts. "My connections to others are radically different now. My world is bigger than before."

We sit next to each other on a park bench adjacent to the St. Francis Yacht Club looking out onto San Francisco Bay. Sailboats bob up and down in the water, scattered throughout a maze of docks that stretch in every direction. It is breathtakingly beautiful.

Arthur grew up in nearby Oakland and sat here most days at lunch, a break from his busy workday schedule. I had visited San Francisco many times but had never been in this place. I am so honored by this treat he is bestowing on me. It feels majestic.

I ask Arthur what made his world so much bigger than before. "Accepting my blindness," says Arthur matter-of-factly. He chooses his words carefully. "Had I not lost my sight, I would never have learned that connection to others helps move us along a trajectory of meeting ourselves. As strange as it may sound, I see so much more now."

CHANGE IN THE FACE OF DISRUPTION

Years earlier, Arthur made a series of *changes* to address his lessening sight, a condition caused by a degenerative eye condition. His response was similar to how many of us respond when we face radically altered circumstances. "Early on, I did not want to tell anyone about my problems with my sight. I wanted to live in the sighted world. I struggled with sightlessness. It took a dozen years for me realize what this was all about," he offers matter-of-factly.

"I was a very outgoing manager at a software company. I knew everybody. And everyone knew me. I joked with the best of them!" he says, smiling. I could instantly sense the kind of energy he brought to his job. "As my sight deteriorated, I started withdrawing. I went out less and less. These were my changes. My world became very small."

Arthur's changes allowed him to maintain some sameness in his self-concept, albeit as a person without the ability to see operating in a sighted world.[1] When we opt for change, we use alterations in particulars to address the disruption, a choice in favor of re-establishing stability in our buffeted sense of self.

Like many of us at times of major crisis, Arthur's choices were cloaked in fear and accompanied by an overwhelming sense of disconnection from the person he had become.

"In a way I kept looking for *me*, before I lost my sight. I looked all through my world as I knew it. The more I looked, the more I could not find me anywhere. It was beyond frightening."

At times of upheaval, change serves as a protective response.[2] With such a response, we reaffirm our self-concept and the stability it offers. In Arthur's case, he made changes, or adjustments, to accommodate his sightlessness. When we reach for such protection, we believe, of course, that this is, in fact, the right thing to do.

Arthur describes to me what came next. "I lost my sense of humor. My confidence evaporated. I lacked an overall direction for my life." The changes Arthur enacted, while he felt they were right-minded at the time, imparted a severe cost on his world.

I found it impossible to connect what I was hearing to the incredible man sitting next to me. This disconnect made me that much more eager to learn how Arthur's changes brought him to the "gift" he described at the outset of our conversation.

TRANSITION IN THE FACE OF DISRUPTION

"I now see that transition had nothing to do with my sight," says Arthur, who marked the start of his eventual transition as an invitation to join a workshop for sight-impaired people. "Transition is about how we see ourselves. Through it, my confidence grew. I set my sights larger and larger." He continues with great emphasis, "My transition was all about seeing value in myself. It was not about losing my sight, per se. It was about who I am."

He smiles broadly and hesitates a moment before going on. I get the sense that he has a surprise for me. "After that workshop, I registered for my first recreational sailing class right here at the Club." I was speechless. I did not know about Arthur's connection to sailing, let alone his connection to this very spot.

"I had to get myself here from my apartment in Oakland twice a week. It forced me to practice with visualization—it is how sight-impaired people, like me, get here from the BART [Bay Area Rapid Transit] station and back. These were steps that helped me, over time, reframe value, my own and what I could offer others."

Arthur was clear: no single step got him to a new place of understanding himself. That expansion occurred over time, iteratively.

"I made plans to meet classmates from my training at places around the city. I took on greater and greater consulting projects, which I did from home. The continuous nature of these steps helped me move forward in important ways." I love how Arthur recognized that he continued to make many changes as he progressed through his transition.

I ask Arthur what he learned from his transition. He replies earnestly, "I learned that my connection to others is not visual. Because I cannot see, my judgment of others is wholly based on interactions. I do not know what you look like or what you are wearing." He hesitates, and then adds, "I feel kind of lucky. I see people, really see people, incredible people whom others look through. It is a gift."

I get goosebumps listening to him.

"The high point happened when I got a new job as a manager at a technology-outsourcing firm just down the street from here. Suddenly, someone else saw value in me. *I* had value." Arthur had been without a consistent source of external validation for years. "I could see it in myself, and other people saw it in me," says Arthur. "It was life changing."

LEADING WITH YOU

Arthur's story underscores the important distinctions between the choice of change and transition in the face of disruption. Transition requires that we actively *choose* to turn up the volume on our own voices. In fact, the one common denominator across *all* transitions is this willingness to deepen our connection to our own truth.

In our world, we use many terms interchangeably to refer to *our truth.* These include voice, inner voice, authentic voice, personal truth, who we are, spirit, essence, personal reality, authentic self, the fullness of who we are, and our wholeness, among others. When I use the term "truth," please keep in mind that I am referring to the fullness of who you are, including that which you only hold in your heart and may never have disclosed to others. "Voice," for our purposes, has nothing to do with speech or audible expressions. Our voices embody who we are, the way we inhabit ourselves and the world, and all that we hold true.

This connection to our truth reveals another important characteristic of transition. Transition *can be* accomplished through a departure, but it is not required. We often believe that we transition by leaving something. We leave a relationship, a way of being, or a city. In fact, departure alone *does not* accomplish a transition. The single requirement for transition is our willingness to turn up the volume on our own voices.

This new lens helps us think about transition in a new way. Transition requires us to *lead with who we are*, a choice that involves identifying and activating our voices and then letting others see, hear, and experience this version of ourselves. Our own understanding of *who we are* can itself be a challenge. Our connection to our own truth can be at varying levels of activation when we encounter a gateway disruption.

I always find it useful to think about this activation in two stages: knowing our truth, and separately being willing to live in alignment with that truth. Both of these stages will be addressed in our work on "how" to respond to disruption in later chapters. For now, I want to share a story that illustrates knowing as opposed to acting in alignment with our truth.

One day, two women approach me at the completion of a seminar for nonprofit leaders that I facilitated in Chicago. One woman is in tears. "I can hear my voice," she starts. "It is screaming at me." While she was connected with who she was, she was frozen in place, afraid of acting in alignment with her voice. "How can I do this?" she asks rhetorically as tears stream down her face. In her mind, the consequences of acting in alignment with her truth were terrifying.

As if on cue, another woman who happened to be standing shoulder distance away turned to share a different relationship with her truth. The second woman put her hand above her eyebrows, mimicking a seafarer searching for a distant land. "Searching! I have not used my voice in thirty years," she says, chuckling. She knew her own journey would begin with taking steps to discover her truth.

Our relationship with our voices is not binary. We do not experience voice as only on or off. Many who choose transition start by *leading* with who they are in small ways prior to making other larger, more visible changes. This iterative approach alters the profile of who can and cannot choose transition. Anyone can opt for transition, including those struggling under a mountain of demands on their time. A small step in the direction of a closer relationship to our voices can translate into asking one more question in a boss's weekly staff meeting or speaking up in a relationship with a combative relative. These small steps can serve as the beginning of a journey similar to Arthur's, who described his own as "life changing."

In the wake of disruption, transition differs from change because it requires us to re-examine our assumptions about who we are and how we make meaning in this world. This path requires us to not only choose but to activate more of our truth. This distinction is important. We can be forced to make many changes in our lives, whereas transition, or leading with who we are, is *always* a choice.

IDENTITY, SELF, AND THE TERMS USED TO DESCRIBE "US"

Throughout this chapter, I have used the terms "who we are," "sense of self," "self-concept," "self-definition," and "identity" interchangeably. I want to clarify two root terms upon which they all rely: *identity* and the *self.*

For our purposes, *identity* is a composite of elements that determine who we are. We are doctors or firefighters or parents or caregivers or nonbinary individuals. We are also energetic and athletic and compassionate and spiritual and introverted and kind. We spend our lifetimes shaping, nourishing, and occupying this composite.

Identity is only part of a greater concept called the *self.* The self adds a number of factors to identity, including our conscious and unconscious mind, as well as our genes and how they interact with one another and our environment.[3] I like to think about identity as our way of making sense of the self.

It is often easier for individuals to get their arms around the term "identity." As such, please keep in mind the following characteristics of identity. First, we are socialized to think of identity as immutable. We love sticky identities. So strong is our allegiance to this thinking that any shifts in identity may be viewed with a skeptical eye. In contrast to this social belief, our identity can repeatedly shift in positive ways over the course of our lives.

Disruption can involve any component of our identity; in fact, disruption can involve one, many, or any part of one component of who we are. For example, your occupation may be firmly set, but your faith and spirituality may be experiencing a disruption. Or you may have a firmly established occupational self, while after the birth of your first child, you have a more nascent identity as it relates to parenting. Either or both can be involved in disruption.

Disruption can involve any component of who you are, regardless of its maturity, centrality, or stage of development. The great news in all of this is that *who we are* has the capacity to shift, again and again, over the course of our lives in many positive ways.

FAVORING CHANGE OVER TRANSITION

We habitually reach for change over transition in the face of disruption. This behavior has nothing to do with the relative ease of one over the other. Changes, while attractive safe havens at times of uncertainty, can be arduous and accompanied by all manner of emotional upheaval. Arthur, like many of us, knew this. He reached for the protection of sameness by making changes, like going out less and less, that attempted to restore stability when he faced unimaginable uncertainty.

In my own journey, I tried change after change, like Arthur, to address my experience of personal upheaval for which I had no name. The changes, which included starting a job search and resigning from a handful of community service activities that I loved, did little to resolve my unnamed conflict. Finally, after a string of unsuccessful changes, I reached for transition as a choice that felt to me like a *last resort*.

I want you to know that I thought I was making all the "right" choices, like many of us at similar junctures, by pursuing change. Nothing worked. About a year after my unraveling at the employee garage when I "borrowed a car," I started in earnest to look for a new job while I took on consulting projects to pay my bills. My job search went on like that for two years. None of the jobs I looked at caught my attention. I could not put my finger on why. There was always something. I had either done the job before, or it did not seem as if I would be working with the right team.

Nearing the end of my rope, I outreached to a former colleague, Phil, for help. He was an unquestionable pooh-bah of Boston's venture capital community. I hoped he would have some ideas for a new job for me since I had spent the bulk of my career in that world.

Phil and I meet for lunch at Legal Seafoods, the venerable Boston-based restaurant chain. We sit at a table not far from the hostess station, above which hangs an enormous plastic fish. The fish, nearly twenty feet long, is frozen in a spirited arc, as if breaching the ocean's surface in a desperate attempt to get away from its captor.

The fish has all my attention. Here I am at a fantastic, long-anticipated lunch and all I can focus on is a suspended plastic fish. There it is, right over my lunch mate's left shoulder.

I am struggling to pay attention to the conversation. A decade earlier, I would have given my right arm to have lunch with Phil. Then, I was a rising entrepreneur in Boston's innovation economy. Now, I am more captivated by the fish than anything my would-be advisor is saying.

What is wrong *with me?* I wonder silently to myself how offended he might be if I make up some excuse and leave. Despite a very real desire to exit, I stay.

I staple myself to my chair and reflexively drop into behaviors that I honed over many years in business. What comes next can only be described as Academy Award worthy.

I draw him out. I listen. I am perky. I prod him with questions about his work. I ask about his point of view on a variety of topics ranging from his industry to our local economy. I puff him up. I congratulate his achievements. I am bubbly.

Another conversation plays out in my head, parallel to this one.

I cannot believe Phil's laziness. He does not extend himself one iota in the conversation. He does not ask any follow-up questions or pursue any points of clarification. I am stunned by this. *Really.*

I cannot help but compare his behavior to my own in similar circumstances. I have sat on the Phil side of the table countless times. I work hard there on behalf of my guest. I offer connections. I wonder aloud about the dreams I hear nestled in their words.

He is perfectly absorbed in his own orbit, a world in which I am seemingly invisible.

This awareness stops me in my tracks. He sees very little—if any-thing at all—of me. I wonder, *What role do I play in this ruse?* I decide to leave that question for later in favor of another more urgent thought.

I feel no connection to him. Even more striking, I cannot see myself anywhere in the world he inhabits.

As he continues to pontificate in response to my questions, my heart sinks further. I consider if Phil is representative of the broader business community. *Am I invisible there too?*

That question is a showstopper. For the last quarter century, I thor-oughly enmeshed myself in this world—a world in which I now ques-tion if I belong.

Right there, in that moment, I feel as if a huge weight descends on my shoulders, throwing me off balance. Whatever is going on with me, I am sure that my answer is somewhere away from here. I see no other option. I feel forced to leave this place I share—or do not share—with Phil.

My internal drama comes screeching to a halt when the waitress arrives to clear our plates. We both decline coffee. I pay the check. We get up to leave.

After our goodbyes, I make it as far as the sidewalk on Boylston Street. I stand there for longer than I had planned. Disoriented. People cut in and out around me.

In the aftermath of that lunch, I am alone in ways I had never been before. Lacking any understanding of what is happening to me, I believe to my core that I am being forced away from the work world I had occupied for so long. Ahead of me is a completely blank slate. The only thing I am certain of is this: I feel as if I am looking for my life.

My turn away from my familiar work world, by some twist of fate, turned me toward transition. At the time, I lacked the vocabulary for and understanding of *change* and *transition* that we all now share. Even without the words, I am grateful for that moment because it started the inquiry that brings me to you.

I also want to acknowledge one important error. I was incorrect about being "forced" to rethink who I was. I made a choice at that moment after the Phil lunch. I chose to re-examine my self-concept even though I lacked the vocabulary at that time to describe it in that fashion. Any of us can make such a choice, one that offers us an opportunity to operate in closer proximity to our truth.

OUR CHOICES

Any choice—let alone a weighty personal one like choosing between change and transition—can feel downright impossible when we are locked in the throes of a gateway disruption. As I experienced at the Phil lunch, we can also feel forced to go in one direction or another—leaving us to believe that we have no choice at all. Given the central role that choice plays in our response to disruption, I want to spend a few minutes on choice and our relationship to it.

PATTERNS IN HOW WE CHOOSE

We all arrive at choice differently. Some arrive with a two-sided ledger in hand, ready to point out the pros and cons of each option in a linear fashion. For others, choice is thoroughly inaccessible, as in, "How can I choose? I do not know what I want yet." Still others lack choice awareness entirely. These folks never really see any times in their lives that warrant a choice.

Three persistent choice-related themes emerged from my research, including a lack of familiarity, equating choice with danger, and a serendipitous on-ramp to choosing.

Many of us lack a *familiarity* with choice. For example, Sydney, a fifty-two-year-old teacher, said of her choices, "I never really made any choices. My dad always wanted me to be a teacher. He did not go to college. He kind of directed my life. Ever since I was a little girl, I was going to be a teacher." Sydney held no animosity toward her dad. Even so, she recognized that at her age, she had little real-world experience with choice.

Others view choice as *dangerous.* Sonali, a twenty-nine-year-old attorney, lacked a comfort level with choice and endeavored to remove choices from her life as much as possible. She described choice in the following fashion: "I became a lawyer so I would not have to make additional choices after deciding on the law. Everything is pretty much laid out for you in that field once you become a lawyer." She shrugged and added, "What can I say? I am bad at choices." Sonali eliminated the need for future choices thanks to her willingness to commit to one. She chose to shelter herself from future choices behind a prescribed identity.

Finally, there are those who deny any relationship at all with choice and instead embrace *serendipity* in their lives. Take Jake, for example. He was deeply connected to his family and the role he played in ensuring their well-being. Even so, he smiled at me devilishly as he related the story of the day he lost his job. "I went home and said to my wife, 'I got the best bad news today.'" This twist of fate that cost him his job gave Jake the permission he would *never* grant himself: the runway to pursue a new career.

Our relationship with choice can easily be linked to many other categories, including judgments about right or wrong choices, and thresholds, like a required minimum age or experience level. Our focus on choice is less about categories or defining a formulaic relationship, as in, "If 'x' happens, do 'y.'" Instead, our work is designed to help you raise your awareness to your relationship with choice and, with that new lens, begin to ask additional questions of yourself.

◈

A REFLECTION: YOUR CHOICES

How do you choose? You may find that you are similar to Sydney, the lifelong teacher who needed to make a choice for the very first time, in her fifties, after decades of embracing her dad's wishes. Or you might be closer to Sonali, who made a single choice of a prescribed identity. Your choice may have involved a move out of your family's home, getting married, joining the Armed Forces, or adopting a child.

This Reflection helps raise your awareness of choices you made in your life and begins to explore "how" you made those choices. We will not pass judgment here, nor are we looking to identify one "right" way to choose.

This Reflection is one of my favorites because it always leads people to important surprises.[4]

Step 1: Take a moment to write down the major choices you have made in your life. Feel free to include milestones like getting your first job, starting a family, beginning a significant relationship, or moving out of your family home. Feel free to list less-tangible choices, like a decision to move away from the tight confines of your spouse's beliefs. Try to include at least three choices in your answer.

Step 2: For each choice listed in Step 1, please write down the other options you considered at the time. Write down as many as you can recall.

For example, I might add, "When I chose to enter college, I also considered going to art school or working at the National Parks in the US West."

Step 3: How would you describe this choice history? It might be useful to answer these prompts:

- Are there patterns to how you have made choices in the past?
- Is there anything about how you made your choices that surprises you?
- Is there one or another choice that you consider a great one? What makes it so?

Step 4: Imagine that you have an opportunity to coach yourself about an upcoming choice. What will you say?

REFLECTION-IN-ACTION

Jasmine, a forty-eight-year-old special education teacher from Chicago, shouts out loud to a small group of people assembled at a focus group, "It has all been about relationships. I have made every decision in my life for relationships." She sounds both triumphant and concerned. The Reflection helped her recognize this choice pattern for the first time. In coaching herself, she says, with a bit of sarcasm, "It might be time to add a few more criteria."

Jasmine's disruption was related to an ongoing argument among her adult siblings over the care needs of her dad, a widower. Would she need to quit her job to take care of her dad? Her relationships were influencing her decision about when and how to leave the Chicago public schools. She had put off looking for a new job for a long time. She wondered if her family relationships had helped her defer that choice. "I've let my relationships with my siblings gate off decisions I need to make for myself," offers Jasmine. "I may not change my decision after this, but I am asking *why* for the first time."

These types of questions can help you access important new insights. For example, Alaine, a highly educated parent of a one-year-old son, recognized through the Reflection that her primary choice criteria had run its course. She worked at a software company dedicated to the fast-growing Internet-of-Things arena. "I was raised to prioritize education," she says, "and to reach as high as I could for achievements related to that." This tried-and-true guardrail was nearing the end of its useful life. "I'm not sure how much further that can take me," she continues. "I'm at a point where I am saying, *What's next?*" Alaine began to see that her earlier criteria were falling away. Their lack of relevance was unsettling, new, and important.

I do not want to overlook those for whom the Choice Reflection is less helpful. Stefan, a senior researcher at a well-known pharmaceutical company in North Carolina, had worked for the same employer for twenty years. He found the exercise very difficult. He reflected on long stretches of his adult life and couldn't recall any choices. He offers, "I've had a series of jobs and, you know, you keep getting more responsibility and your salary goes up and this and that happens and all of a sudden, you know, it gets harder to tell people where you're at."

His observation was simple and stark. "After I joined the company, this was years ago, I did not choose. I started there because it was a job, and I needed one. Once there, I was on track. I did not make any choices. They were made for me." Even though Stefan's Choice Reflection was relatively sparse, he learned a great deal about his relationship with choice from the exercise.

Your Choice Reflection will not give you an "answer," nor will it stand in judgment of your past choices. Instead, it raises your awareness of the behaviors related to choice that walk with you in responding to a disruption.

Our comfort level with choice will play a role in how we respond to disruptions. Re-examining the assumptions upon which you architect your beliefs about who you are is a choice. Those willing to act on their own behalf and make such a choice embark on a new kind of journey, a positive, enlivening, life-changing course.

◈

WHAT ARE WE REALLY CHOOSING?

Change and transition represent different choices in the wake of disruption. Changes reaffirm our self-concept and involve the pursuit of alterations or variations.

Transition invites us to explore shifts in our self-concept. It is not about departures or turning away from something; instead, it is about turning toward a more complete version of who we are. When we choose transition, we are activating something important: *ourselves.* Transition invites us to turn on one of the most powerful tools we have at our disposal: our unique, irreplaceable truth. We alone have the capacity to choose this path. No one can force us to do so.

If we choose transition, we re-examine our assumptions about who we are and how we make meaning in the world. This choice involves calling upon more of our capacity as we make our way along an unknown but certain path. The choice of transition rests upon our willingness to not only establish a deeper connection to our truth but also to let others hear, see, and experience more of who we are. In addition to all of this, the choice of transition enables something else that is critically important in our lives. The choice of transition enables transformational growth.

3

Choosing Growth

The lens of disruption offers us a new on-ramp to growth similar to its contribution to our understanding of the difference between change and transition. Audrey, thirty-four, underscores this contribution when she comes up to talk with me after an event I led in Morristown, New Jersey. As she starts to talk, she has a look of puzzled intrigue on her face.

"Ever since I was a little girl, I dreamed of being in the military," she says. "I lived the dream. I became a sergeant." After serving for six years, Audrey was diagnosed with a cardiac rhythm abnormality while she was stationed abroad. She was immediately deemed unfit for duty and sent home.

Once home, she worked hard to get her arms around the changes in her health and struggled with incapacitating bouts of depression. Eventually, she decided to get certified to be a teacher. Once complete, she worked hard to restore some measure of normalcy.

"It's been nearly a decade since this all happened." She adds, "I still do not know how to think about myself outside of the military.

"What if this was all *growth*?" She asks in a tone of resignation and fascination.

Our work in this chapter will address Audrey's question and sharpen our understanding of the type of growth available to those who choose transition in the wake of a gateway disruption. We will revisit our understanding of choice and test our beliefs about the powerful life-altering potential of growth.

LINKING CHOICE AND GROWTH

Our choice of transition enables transformative growth. This type of growth occurs when we shift the assumptions upon which we architect our sense of self. For example, Audrey may have anchored her beliefs about *who she was* on her participation in the military. Once she left the service, she found it difficult to reconcile who she was outside of it. Transformative growth is a process that works to alter, update, and expand our sense of self while at the same time addressing the role played by prior expressions of our our identity, which in Audrey's case was the military. This type of growth can be confusing, difficult, hopeful, and empowering.

Transformational growth is a process during which we shift the inputs—the beliefs, values, and expectations—upon which we build our self-concept.[1] This shifting of inputs from one to another brings us closer to our truth. Carole, a fifty-three-year-old physician's assistant who was recently widowed, joins me for coffee in Pasadena, California, to share a story of her growth journey. "I am so very different now. I finally got to the point of understanding the value in accessing more of *me* and exercising *my* voice. It's been a game changer."

Carole describes a year of major upheaval in her life and her subsequent choice of transition. She says, "We were focusing on the kids, our lives. My husband, Luis, and I married young. Our marriage had not worked out the way either of us had envisioned." She pauses, as if reflecting on the weight of sharing something so personal. "All of a sudden, we lost him in a car accident." She and her three college-age sons were heartbroken.

"Luis's death kind of laid the groundwork for my choice. Without it, I would not have been so aware of the need to re-examine my beliefs." This awareness prompted Carole's growth.

"Luis's death, while heartbreaking, didn't serve as my disruption. Even though I am sure everyone around me believed that was so. It was not until a year later when my eldest son was considering job offers after graduation that it hit me. I needed to parent differently." It was an unexpected turn.

"My old assumptions about the family living close by were not working," she says, explaining how she tried to use long-established beliefs about parenting during a time when her son was considering relocation. "My new thinking required me to be more transparent than ever before. I did not want my relationship with my son to suffer because of this move, particularly after the loss my family had already endured."

Similar to Carole's experience, transformational growth begins when we become aware of the assumptions we carry about who we are. Awareness in and of itself does not equate to growth, however. Growth requires that we take additional steps. These steps, which we will learn how to navigate in the upcoming chapters, ask us to re-examine, refine, and potentially disengage from the beliefs, values, and expectations we carry, as well as create new ones and learn to live in alignment within them. Such growth is an act of creation, a process of coming into our own voices.[2] This process yields something important: a new self-concept anchored by what holds value and meaning *to us*.

Transforming our self-concept offers us a fundamentally new way to occupy the many roles we accrue over our lifetime. Most adults create their initial self-concept as if "filling in a paint-by-numbers canvas, creating ourselves within the outline of stories, wishes, and mindsets projected onto to us."[3] I love this analogy offered by author Sue Monk Kidd of her own transformational journey. For some, building our self-concept within the lines can extend throughout a lifetime, creating comfort, adventure, and safety. For others, those same lines can lead to an awareness of gaps, as in Carole's case, or even disconnection and numbness. When externally informed self-concepts prove restrictive, transformational growth helps us de-layer what was projected onto us by others and re-create our self-concept based more closely upon that which holds value and meaning to us. Such shifts lead to an enlivening, liberating, optimistic, and updated self-definition.

AN ILLUSTRATION

I like to think about transformational growth as being similar to walking along a winding path and repeatedly changing my glasses as I do so. Imagine that the lens material in each new pair of glasses is made of different inputs. Some inputs are external to us, and others are closer to our hearts.

If we stay with this analogy, the path itself can be thought of in parts. On the earliest parts of the path, all of the glasses we pick up have lenses that are formed by external influences. At the midpoint of the path, the glasses available to us have lenses made of inputs that are internally sourced or self-defined. At the latter parts of the path, the glasses have lenses formed by the beliefs, values, and expectations that transcend any one individual and connect our self-concept to the harmony and beneficence of all beings.

Transformational growth allows us to progress along the path, ensuring that our sense of self benefits from new and alternative influences along the way.

A CASE STUDY

Margaret's story illustrates a progression along this path. She invited me to talk with her at her tidy mountainside cabin in the foothills of the Wasatch Range, just outside of Salt Lake City, Utah. A mutual friend put us in touch because Margaret was toying with what to do about an unexpected early retirement brought on by the pandemic.

Margaret surprises me as we start to talk because she has little interest in talking about her job crisis. To start, I ask her to describe transition.

"Transition does have pain with it, or hurt with it, or sadness with it, *something*. It is saying goodbye to a lot. You are saying goodbye to what you thought would happen. So, you have got to get past what you expected, the expectations. But on the other side of that choice is this fantastic new world." She pauses and adds, "It's hard, but it's worth it."

LOOKING THROUGH EXTERNALLY DEFINED LENSES

"I came from an extremely dysfunctional family," Margaret starts. "Alcoholism. An abusive father. Physical brutality." Margaret's voice trails off as she shares the weightiness of these early influences.

"I am an army brat. We moved every two years when I was a kid." She is the eldest daughter of seven children. "You never knew if the kids in the next town were going to like you," she says flatly. "All I wanted to do was to get out. I moved out at eighteen. I got married at nineteen." Even with her firm resolve, the marriage did not work out as she had planned.

"It should have been so simple," she says softly. "I made him unhappy. He made me unhappy." If only life could be that simple. "I was a good Catholic girl. Marriage was forever. I had no reason to leave him." She pauses a moment and adds, "*Unhappy?* That is a fancy problem."

Margaret's story mirrored the common characteristics of early adulthood, a period during which our self-concept is formed by adopting definitions and expectations of those around us. These *external* influences can include our families, our occupation, our religious affiliation, the community in which we live, our intimate relationships, our friends, the schools we attend, our racial, ethnic, sexual, and gender affiliations, and much more. At the earliest stages of growth, we anchor our self-concept on these values and beliefs we uncritically—and often unknowingly—adopt from those around us.

As Margaret tried to make sense of her unhappy marriage, a traumatic event hit her family. Her next oldest sibling, John, died in a skiing accident. Margaret was twenty-four. She confides in me that the accident happened not far from where we sit talking. "John was magnetic. Everybody loved him. He was kind and the smartest of us all."

She gets up from the couch where we are sitting to get a beautiful silver mirror from the mantle. I can see it is a compact that folds into its own thin case. "It was John's," she says as she hands it to me. Closed, it fits in the palm of my hand. "The mirror was always on his bureau no matter where we lived as children."

LOOKING THROUGH SELF-DEFINED LENSES

"I started questioning everything after John's death," says Margaret after she sits back down. "I can remember saying to a cousin at the time, 'How long is this going to hurt so much?'" Margaret's pain was tied not only to John's passing but also to the questions she began to ask herself.

"When he died, I had no self-confidence. I was so afraid. I was convinced that I could not do anything," says Margaret.

Margaret's growing awareness prompted her to begin taking small steps. "These steps were hard," she recalls. She went back to school at night while working a full-time job.

"When I first started taking classes, and they were not difficult, I never thought it was me. I thought they were just not difficult courses." Margaret discovered there was more to this. "I was always told, 'You're not very bright,'" she says flatly. "When I did well in later courses, it was just stunning that, you know, I could do them.

"I kept taking steps. I worked hard. I found out that I could do things better than my husband. Over time, I realized I was the more responsible person in the relationship and that I was okay. I was not stupid." It took her ten years to finish her degree.

"Graduating from college when you're told your whole life you're not very bright was big." She continues softly, "My marriage ended when I was thirty-four, shortly after I graduated. It was a long time coming. When he walked out the door, I felt a tremendous weight lift off my shoulders."

Like Margaret's experience, transformative growth occurs in a series of iterative steps. The steady nature of these steps alters our behavior, providing more acceleration to our growth. In aggregate, these steps enable us to know ourselves through our own voices instead of knowing ourselves through the values, beliefs, and expectations of others that are projected onto us.

I want to caution us not to interpret *self-defined* as similar to *self-absorbed*. When we operate through a self-defined sense of self, as Margaret learned, we reconstruct our relationships with others to be more genuine and reflective of who *we* are.

I ask Margaret how it feels to come into her own voice. "I started to believe—slowly at first—that nothing was going to get in my way."

LOOKING TO OTHERS IN A NEW WAY

Margaret's unexpected job loss in the early days of the pandemic brought her to another choice. Thanks to her earlier positive experience with growth, she is resolute. "I want to keep growing. I am not ready to retire."

Even so, she is uncertain about how to proceed. "I am not sure what I want to do," Margaret offers questioningly. "What is surprising me about all this has nothing to do with the job. It is about my relationships with my siblings." She stops as if surprised to be saying it out loud. "I did not expect to be stuck on *this*." Margaret stepped in years earlier to financially help her brother and sister-in-law, as part of her role in the family as the one who watched out for everyone.

"The most surprising part of all this is how painful and unwelcome it is to be questioning this part of who I am." Margaret pauses and continues carefully. "I do not know who I am without taking care of everyone." She says, "While I will never leave that part of me entirely, I need to figure out where that line is."

Margaret's growing awareness extended beyond her relationships with her siblings. "There is something about community I am drawn to," says Margaret. She began experimenting with new directions while she sorted out the bits with her siblings. "I do not know what it means yet. I am volunteering at a veterans' center in town. It reminds me of when I was a kid living on base," she adds as a giant smile lights up her face.

"Everyone always helped one another. On Saturdays in the fall, I remember there being snow-tire brigades. The whole base got together and put on everyone's snow tires, particularly those who had family members deployed. We took care of everyone."

Margaret's growth expressed itself as a broadening awareness of her voice and an increasing connection to others. Those who progress similarly learn to set their expectations for and definition of who they are by expanding beyond self-defined beliefs and integrating with more collective beliefs. Margaret was experiencing a characteristic of growth that William James, the founder of modern psychology, started exploring in the late 1800s. He said of this growth stage, "We experience union with something larger than ourselves, and in that union find our greatest peace."[4]

EMBRACING GROWTH

Transformative growth greatly increases our ability to withstand uncertainty. By embarking on such a path, we become less susceptible to unexpected twists and turns because we move beyond a self-concept that relies primarily on external influences. When our self-concept is updated with that which is more internally anchored, we deepen our connection to who we are and fortify our ability to navigate unsettled times.

I ask Margaret to offer a final word on growth. "I learned a lot about myself," she says confidently and then adds, "You have to say goodbye to whatever your dreams were that you thought were going to happen and move on to the *new* ones." She pauses for an instant, smiles broadly, and finishes, "It's going to be great."

A CLOSER PROXIMITY

Growth offers tremendous value for those willing to choose transition and undertake a transformative journey. There is no "type" to transformative growth; we do not go on one type of journey if our disruption involves a job loss and another type of journey if our disruption involves the birth of another child. The process of transformation is the same regardless of the initiating circumstances that preceded our choice.

Through transformative growth, we unlearn beliefs and behaviors that can diminish or marginalize our voices. This step allows us to distance ourselves from self-limiting narratives. For example, Margaret grew to challenge her narrative of not being "bright." She was surprised, as so many of us are at similar junctures, when she became aware of the incorrect nature of this story that she had carried since childhood.

Our voices gain strength thanks to the iterative nature of growth. No single step alone is responsible for igniting our confidence or increasing our self-awareness. It is the dynamic of taking a step and then another in favor of gaining a closer proximity to our truth that changes our outlook and behavior. Said Margaret, "I kept taking steps."

Transformative growth brings us in closer proximity to our truth. It invites us to live in alignment with what holds value and meaning to us. In the upcoming chapters, we will explore the steps required for such a progression and the gifts available for all those who progress in this fashion. For now, please keep in mind that gateway disruptions invite us to make choices that create a deeper intimacy with who we are.

◆

A REFLECTION: YOUR GROWTH

Have you ever embarked on a transformative journey? Are you ready for one now?

Step 1: Have you ever embarked on a path of growth? Please describe your experience(s) with growing.

Step 2: Circle any experiences listed in Step 1 that you believe were transformative.

Keep in mind, transformational growth is a process during which we shift the inputs—the beliefs, values, and expectations—upon which we architect our self-concept.

Step 3: How did it feel to navigate transformative growth? Did it differ from any other growth experiences in your life?

REFLECTION-IN-ACTION

Justine, thirty-eight, started college as a bioengineering major with a dream to run her own lab. Even so, she begins her story of growth with heartache. "I always thought I was not good enough to pursue my dreams. I never had enough confidence in myself. I think I am ready now."

Justine had not worked outside of the home for twelve years. "I studied hard in college and interned at a prestigious lab in the Los Angeles area. I was so afraid. My own insecurities kept me from pursuing my dream. I landed a good job teaching science in the public school system. I was never satisfied. I hated it.

"The time for growth is right now for me," says Justine with conviction. "Feeling not good enough and not having confidence in myself has led to a powerlessness that is hard to admit to anyone, let alone myself." Justine joined my research thanks to a need to re-enter the workforce that was prompted by her husband's job loss. "In a way, I am glad about my husband's job. He lost it six months before the pandemic. It whacked me out of balance. This is not only about his job. It is bigger. It is time. This is about me."

Justine's firm resolve did not eliminate the formidable emotional upheaval she encountered. "This is terrifying and stressful. Some days I am so ashamed to be looking at entry-level positions. My former classmates are now the hiring managers! That part is embarrassing and beyond upsetting." Justine's pressing financial circumstances added focus to her search, but she knew it was about something in addition to paying the bills. "I am not sure where this will lead. I do not think I could live with myself if I do not try."

Justine's intentions situated her at the on-ramp of transformational growth and the unparalleled gifts available to those who choose it.

◆

A POWERFUL AWARENESS

Justine made a courageous choice to step toward uncertainty. Those who make such a choice gain access to the benefits of growth as they make their way in an iterative fashion along the path. Those who do are greeted with gifts continuously all along the way. The benefits of transformative growth are not gated off until we cross a finish line sometime in the future. One such gift—validation—plays a critical role as we envision and create new self-concepts. I was incredibly fortunate to experience such affirmation on my own journey.

After my lunch with Phil and the disconnection I experienced toward my work, I began a transformative journey at forty-eight years old. For the first time since my early twenties, I faced a blank slate with respect to my career. I was thrashing about. One day I would look for jobs, and the next, I was dreaming about changing the world. The only certainty I held was that I did not know where I was going. I had no five-year plan, no overarching goal. I gave myself permission to be in this state of not knowing. I tried and tried to ignore those around me who advocated the need for a plan. I engaged my curiosity while standing arm in arm with the uncertainty.

Like Margaret, who took courses, I took a first step in a direction that interested me. I created a blog to document my journey. I really liked writing the blog but quickly convinced myself that I needed to add experiences beyond my own story to make the writing rich and meaningful to readers. That belief contributed to the first focus groups I talked about in Chapter 1. It was a first step. It was not my last.

I took a step, learned from it, took a bigger step, learned from it, took an even bigger step, and learned from it. I kept turning in a direction that felt right and taking the next step. First in small ways, then in larger and larger ways. I did that repeatedly for three years while asking myself important questions. There was never a point where I knew what would be next. I got momentum from this step-by-step approach. So much so that when I submitted a proposal for my first book and got a rejection, I was unphased. I submitted it to another publisher straightaway and landed it.

These iterative steps, combined with questions, created something unstoppable. They helped me connect to *me* in a new way. I gained confidence and unlocked a personal power that I had previously only glimpsed. This journey was freeing, enlivening, and magical. Out of the process came a reconstituted professional identity. I became an expert on personal and organizational transformation, a job that includes speaking, facilitating workshops, hosting a podcast, consulting, and undertaking additional research. Surprisingly, this focus linked to work on business transformation that I had done nearly continuously since I got out of college.

There was something else, too. I encountered others who saw value in my newly updated self-concept. I vividly remember the first time this affirmation occurred with the arrival of a note from Kaitlyn, a forty-two-year-old mother of teenage twins from Seattle, Washington, who attended a global webinar I hosted.

> I just attended your webinar and can't thank you enough. Your session was such a validation of what I've been trying to put into words that it brought me to tears. I now have 'permission' to feel excited, terrified, and demoralized all at once. I have experienced many key events in my life—marriage, death, divorce, infertility, miscarriage, childbirth, and sudden illness. None of those were disruptive in the manner that professional boredom and job loss—seven weeks ago—have been. After listening to your session, I am now aware that I have been in transition for more than just the past seven weeks. It started two years ago when I realized my personal values differed in fundamental ways from those around me.
>
> I am very grateful to hear that I'm not crazy. You talked about exactly where I find myself today: overwhelmed, uncertain, anxious, and excited. Thank you for suggesting that this phase of growth is both normal and appropriate.

Kaitlyn helped me see something new about my own journey: other people saw value in this newly refined me. I want to be clear: at this stage of growth, we are not looking to others for self-definition, only to affirm new ways in which we envision ourselves. Without such sources of feedback, our growth can falter. Kaitlyn also helped me understand something profound: I loved creating a space for others to connect more closely with who they are.

In spite of these wins, my journey was far from over. I had the confidence to keep going, but not because I magically had a destination in mind. I had something more powerful. I had a newly expanded connection to my truth.

A NEW CONVERSATION

Our choice of transition enables transformative growth, a step-by-step process that leads us to update the beliefs upon which we architect our sense of self. This growth invites us to anchor our self-concept on that which holds value and meaning *to us* instead of on the beliefs and expectations we often unknowingly adopt from the people and circumstances around us. Growth teaches us to ask new questions about ourselves. Once we embark on such a path, we learn to greet ourselves and the world differently.

Transformational growth's most profound gift is its ability to connect us in a deeper way to who we are. As we progress through this process, we learn to rely on our voices more consistently. We increase our ability to withstand uncertainty. We access more of our capacity. And we expand our comfort level with not knowing.

Transformation represents a beginning, in earnest, of a new conversation with ourselves.

II

SETTING THE STAGE

4

Meeting Resistance

This is an important moment in our discussion about disruption. In fact, it is all I can do not to roll out the confetti machine and ask you about your favorite music. I hope you agree that your decision to explore transformational growth warrants such a celebration. However, as you may already know, it is impossible to choose transition without encountering resistance.

Arya, a fifty-five-year-old cancer survivor, shared a lighthearted story about her work on reimagining her identity. It sums up resistance perfectly. "After ten years with the same organization, twenty-two years in the same house, and thirty-three years with the same man, I'm ready!" Then she adds, "If I could just get past my own fears and insecurities!" Arya, like many of us, was aware of forces that stood in her way, making it difficult to proceed as she intended.

Our work in this chapter will focus on emotions that can create opposition to our choice of growth. We will center on increasing our awareness of emotions and their influence on us. This exploration is a valuable precursor to the later chapters in which we will learn how to reframe emotions that attempt to work against us as we grow.

My goal with this chapter is to reposition emotions as an integral part of our path to establishing a deeper connection to who we are. Our emotions can serve as an oracle, not an obstacle, to our success.

WHAT IS RESISTANCE?

Resistance is anything in our experience that impedes our progress
in a desired direction. It can take many forms, including emotional,
physical, physiological, energetic, and cognitive. And it shows up in
a variety of ways. An unsupportive spouse. A feeling of unworthiness.
A physical or developmental limitation. Self-doubt. Too little time.
Sudden success. A toxic work environment. The lack of a credential.
Financial obligations. Adverse childhood experiences. Anxiety. Fear.
Debilitating back pain. Listlessness. Boredom. Sleeplessness. Spending
too much time alone.

We can be aware of our resistance, or it can operate in a slightly more
undercover fashion. Think about James, a forty-four-year-old attorney
who became an entrepreneur after years of dreaming about such a
move. Within a month of starting his own business, he was overcome
with crushing back pain. This physical onslaught made it impossible
for him to pursue his goal as originally planned. James was well aware
of the pain but stopped short of considering it as symptomatic of his
resistance to decoupling from his familiar way of being. Without such
awareness, resistance can work to keep us stuck in place despite our
very real desire to go forward.

Resistance is highly individual and can occur at any time throughout
our transformative journey. For example, we can meet resistance ini-
tially as we consider whether or not to pursue a transition in the wake
of a disruption. We can meet it at the beginning of our transformative
journey as we disengage from long-held expectations about who we are.
Or we can meet it well into our process as we create and refine new self-
expressions. This continuous relationship with resistance is contrary to
widely held beliefs.

Many of us think about resistance as a hurdle to overcome. We work
to eradicate it, often deferring other activities until we do. In this vein,
we dream about a time in the future when we will have worked hard
enough, or smart enough, or long enough, or will have saved enough
money, to arrive at a "Resistance-Free Zone," or RFZ.

I hate to be the one to tell you this, but RFZs do not exist. Resistance behaves like the popular game Whac-A-Mole. No sooner do
we have one form of opposition solved than another one springs up.

Think about your neighbor who has been stressed for years and finally announces that she has paid the last tuition bill for her third college student. Her euphoria is met by her aging father's exploding health care needs. Thanks to the persistent nature of resistance, our work invites us to consider another path for dealing with such opposition.

Our goal is not to eliminate, overcome, or ignore resistance but to learn how to be successful in its presence. Resistance can play a surprisingly critical role in our journey forward if we are willing to bring new thinking to it.

EMOTIONS AS RESISTANCE

Emotional resistance is a form of opposition that occurs when emotions, like anger or fear, impede our progress in a desired direction. We will use the term "emotion" as a shorthand for the feelings, sensations, responses, and emotions that are a part of our experience. Emotional resistance is as powerful, common, and equally influential when it appears as anxiety as when it appears as perfectionism.

Emotions, for our purposes, are a collection of responses designed at their most basic level to maintain life. We all know the primary emotions, including fear, anger, surprise, disgust, happiness, and sadness.[1] We also know emotions as a variety of other responses, including embarrassment, guilt, jealousy, pride, tension, anxiety, shame, regret, self-doubt, relief, isolation, and many others. I have always loved neuroscientist Antonio Damasio's description of emotions: "They are induced in the brain and play out in the theatre of the body."[2]

What follows is a list of emotions that are common in our experience of resistance (Figure 4.1).[3] Which ones are familiar to you?

Denise, a sixty-one-year-old store manager at a supermarket in Maine, brought the experience of emotional resistance to life in her story about finding her way in growth.

"Who am I if I am not me?" asks Denise when we sit down to talk about her recent disruption. Her employer, a major national supermarket chain, reorganized, leaving Denise without a job. She has a raspy voice and a straight-talking manner.

Figure 4.1. Common Emotions.

"I am devastated. I did not know that my job was going to be affected by this [reorganization]. I worked there for twenty years. It was a total shock."

I ask Denise to describe her emotions. "I am full of anxiety. I mean, this is scary! You know, all the emotions are here. Mostly, I feel worthless and insecure." She takes a breath and adds, "The question of who I am scares the bejesus out of me."

"You do not feel like you are in control," offers Denise. "It sort of hits some very emotional chords." Denise was quick to link her loss with the sadness and grief she experienced over her husband's death eight years earlier. He passed away after a short battle with pancreatic cancer. "It is like losing him again. It is a pretty scary thing, you know, the concept of stepping into that void."

In spite of her raging emotions, growth is the only option Denise is willing to consider. "I never let fear win before," she says patently. "Why should I start now?"

Denise had made a choice, an important one. Her choice of growth did not extinguish the very real resistance she experienced. She was resolute, however, that it was not going to stop her.

RESISTANCE ON OUR JOURNEY

Emotional resistance, as Denise knew, can be a formidable companion as we progress along a path of transforming our self-concept. Rashid, a father of three in his late forties, found himself treading water in a sea of emotions both immediately after a layoff and continually as he made his way along a path of reimagining his identity.

"To be honest, the last two and a half years were incredibly stressful. Our department merged with another. It did not go very well. We were being re-assigned constantly. Everything was a number-one priority. No one could be successful in that. I was happy to get out."

I ask Rashid how it felt to be part of the downsizing. "Don't get me wrong. There was shock," says Rashid. "Like, 'Wow, this actually happened to me?'" He had spent eighteen years at the company on what he described as a slow and steady upward pace. "I know the drill. At sixty-one, my dad was laid off after working for twenty-three years at a huge technology company here in the Valley. But I did not really think it would happen to me at forty-six." His voice reveals his surprise at this unexpected twist.

"When it happened, I came home incredibly relieved. I immediately knew it was an opportunity to pursue something that I wanted to do for a long time. The very next day, at 9 a.m., I started to investigate opportunities in the coastal management field. It is an area I always loved in school. I got the fire in my belly again. It was exciting. It got me going." Rashid viewed the layoff as an opportunity, even though the job loss was unexpected.

The exuberance of his first day quickly dissipated. "I have good days and bad days, and to be honest, that has persisted."

I ask about the emotions that appear more regularly for him during this time. "Fear," says Rashid without even needing a second to think about a response. "My fear is all related to financial concerns." He continues, "We are lucky. We have always had a two-income strategy. We did a budget. We did not even know it, but we can survive basically on one salary. We are very simple. We do not do a lot of crazy stuff. We realized we can do this." Even though he knew on one level that he had no practical near-term financial risk, he could not shake his fear.

While Rashid's fear expressed itself as financial worry, others in my research experienced fear in different ways. The chart that follows, derived from my research, highlights some additional ways fear shows up as we grow (Figure 4.2).

In addition to fear, Rashid reflexively overlaid meaning onto his experience of emotions. For example, when we feel sad, we add meaning to the experience of sadness, with thoughts like, "There must be something wrong with me." This behavior is a self-limiting reflex common to many of us.

"On my worst days, I am thinking, *What am I doing?* I am not providing for my family." He continues, "I go through these cycles where my self-talk is damaging. I say, *Okay, I am forty-six, I have three kids, a dog, a mortgage, and a wife who is working really hard. What am I doing? Is this irresponsible of me?* Sometimes, I think, *Seriously, just get a job, any job, just get a job.*"

Rashid leans closer to me and says in a hushed tone, "I am facing a major event with all these emotions. I try to be positive, but it is hard."

Figure 4.2.   How Fear Shows Up.

I ask him to give me an example of this difficulty. He replies, "*Can I do this? Should I do this?* What makes this so hard is that when I think about my decision from that perspective, I can go into a dark place. I knew it would be tough, but the ups and the downs can set me back."

Rashid continued to coach three soccer teams, one for each son, during this process. It was not easy. He felt judged by a public perception of his decision. "I know that parents are all talking about me on the other side of the field," he shares. His words reveal the stress he carries thanks to what he perceives as the judgmental gaze of others. "I'm viewed as 'damaged goods.' I cannot help but think, *Did I fail? How did I ever think I could restart my career at this stage?* Then I circle back to, *What is* wrong *with me?*"

Rashid skillfully applied meaning to these emotions. "I have a house and a family and all that goes with it, and then I go get laid off. I start losing confidence.

"One of the hardest parts of the whole thing is fighting off judging myself. On the outside, everyone wants you to be positive, but it is not all smooth sailing. It is hard to explain to people. It is an emotional hodgepodge. Part of it is embarrassing."

Emotions—in one form or another—were Rashid's constant companion. He finishes, "I know if I give up, it will never happen. I have to stay with it, but it is a lot harder than I ever imagined."

Emotions play a fundamental role in growth, as Rashid experienced first-hand. If we leave them unaddressed, they will lead the way. We can, however, reframe our experience of them and, in doing so, add knowledge and momentum to our journey.

EMOTIONS AND GROWTH

Emotions play a starring role in our experience of disruption and growth, although we can easily misinterpret their contributions. Nearly everyone on the planet, like Rashid, can share a list of emotions that they have experienced at times of uncertainty. What we may miss is appreciating the role that emotions play in growth.

Emotions mobilize to keep us safe when we knowingly disengage from the stability of a familiar expression of who we are. Rashid battled fear about money as he stepped away from a career identity he nourished for eighteen years. In fact, he could not shake the fear even though he knew on a rational level that he had no near-term financial risk. Emotions may show up as counterproductive to what we intend to do.

I always imagine this type of response as our emotions serving as a cautious friend who asks, "Are you sure?" as we disengage from a familiar expression of who we are and continue along a path of growth. When emotions behave in this fashion, they can easily distract us, distort our understanding of what is occurring, send us on detours, and otherwise thwart our ability to move forward.

As we said, we reflexively add meaning to the presence of an emotion, adding to its oppositional effectiveness. Rashid referenced this type of behavior throughout our conversation with phrases like, "What is wrong with me?" and "I'm viewed as damaged goods."

Society aids in this ruse by teaching us to reach for a preferred emotion while overwriting more authentic ones. For example, social pressures invite us to lean toward an emotion like happiness instead of fear. While many of us authentically experience happiness, if we overwrite our own emotions in favor of a predetermined "desirable" one, what we rely on is known as an emotional bypass.[4] Think about a neighbor who shares how sad she feels now that her house is an empty nest, only to correct herself an instant later with, "I know I am not supposed to feel that way." An emotional bypass is a form of resistance that can, over time, teach us to distrust our own emotions.

Emotions stand ready, if we ask them, to add momentum and clarity to our progress. Keep in mind that an emotion, like sadness, can appear as spontaneously as a firefly on a June evening as we embark on a path of growth. It is there—protecting us—hoping we make an informed choice.

◆

A REFLECTION: NAMING YOUR RESISTANCE

Have you ever encountered emotional resistance? This chapter's Reflection asks you to bring your awareness to emotions, in whatever form, that may be present as you consider reimagining your sense of self. There is no judgment or right or wrong answer regarding your experience of emotions. Our goal is simply to name that which is present for you.

>   **_Step 1:_** Think about a time of growth in your life. What emotions were active for you at that time?
>
>   *Note, for our purposes, we use the term "emotions" to refer to the feelings, responses, sensations, and emotions that occur in our experience.*
>
>   **_Step 2:_** How did the above-listed emotions influence you?

REFLECTION-IN-ACTION

Wanda, thirty-eight, a Los Angeles native and graphic artist, was devastated as she told me about how she left her marriage. She and I met at a little coffee shop at the base of Runyon Canyon in Los Angeles.

She was surprised by how easy it was to name her emotions. "I feel invalidated, worthless, and broken. I am not sure what is next," she says. Her husband walked out after seventeen years of marriage. He told her he was in love with another man. "Confused. And angry. I cannot believe this is happening to us. To *me*." She looks away and then back at me. "I really have no words. Everything I thought I knew is wrong. I am fragile. I have never felt so alone." She stops for a minute, then adds, shaking her head, "How did I not see this?"

Wanda has a slightly tougher time answering the question about influence. "Things had not been going well for a long time," she says. "I withdrew. Simple as all that. I withdrew from family, from friends. I do not know if it was resistance, but I felt ashamed. *I told you so*, is a phrase that keeps playing in my head. I do not know what it means. I always knew there was something. I ignored my instincts. I guess I just kept going, hoping things would get better."

Wanda is silent for a long time, then adds, with pursed lips, "How could I have ignored my instincts for so long?"

◆

MOVING BEYOND BARRIERS

Once we learn to bring our awareness to our emotions and consider their influence, we can move on to the important work of reframing them, a technique we will learn in Chapter 6. To reframe is to bring fresh thinking to something familiar. Reframing is essential to our success with growth because it helps us alter our experience of emotions. Reframing emotions also allows us to ask important new questions of ourselves.

My own story with emotional resistance offers clues as to the usefulness of such reframing.

"Now that you are an author, how do you think differently about your career?" asks a woman who stood with the first question at a "Meet the Author" event in New York City. I was speaking at the local chapter of the Harvard Business School Women's Alumni Network. As at most events, the audience's questions came right after my prepared remarks.

Upon hearing her question, tears instantly well up in the corners of my eyes. *Here? Now? Are you kidding?* I say to myself, admonishingly. I struggle to keep the tears at bay.

"Your question is funny to me, in a way," I reply, hoping no one can see my tears. "I have never used the word 'author' to describe myself." The irony of my response is not lost on me, given the event's title.

I do not have the luxury of dwelling on what is happening at that moment. One hundred people sit facing me, ready for me to answer their questions.

I get a moment to myself an hour later. Reaching for my coat behind the beautifully lit stage, I wonder, *Why the tears?*

No easy answers come. Is there something about *here?* With this audience? I am ashamed I cried. These people are my peers. Aren't they? I had never cried before on a stage. This thinking quickly gives way to a surprising question.

What right do I have to be an author? *Wow.* That comes out of nowhere. And it really stings. I did write a book that was published by a major publishing house. Aren't I an author? The term feels loftier than the space I have the right to occupy.

I wonder about this. Shame instantly pops to mind. Shame and I have been besties for my entire life.

I ask myself about shame, and without hesitation, my mind toggles to a long-ago place. I grew up in a household where I learned to work hard, but words of kindness or encouragement were never spoken.

"Don't make waves!" was the most supportive phrase that came my way. It stood for so much: do not speak your mind, do not let others see you, do not draw attention to yourself, don't, don't, don't.

That memory helps me consider my presence on that stage, any stage, as an act of defiance against being shamed for who I was or for my ideas. Could the tears be an oddly played high five?

I smile a bit at this thought as I make my way to the elevators and down to the sidewalk in front of the building. I make waves *every day*—much to the chagrin of those in my childhood home. I always have. Are my tears a final wave goodbye to that smothering retort I learned when I was so young?

I hold this new thinking in my heart. Reframed, my awareness of shame invites me to reach farther. I am no longer held by it as I access a belief in myself and in my enduring ability to use my voice. It reinforces a path I am on instead of one that is holding me back. I am triumphant as an author. Instead of asking, *What is wrong with me?* my new awareness prompts me to ask, *What is next?*

WALKING WITH EMOTIONS

Emotions play a vital role in our growth journey. While they mobilize to keep us safe as we grow beyond familiar expressions of ourselves, they also offer us important clues, like my response to taking the stage as an author, a defiant high five in opposition to the shame I learned in my childhood home. These clues can add clarity and momentum to our journey.

Part of an emotion's value comes in the form of questions we ask ourselves in their presence. While the accuracy of our answers to these questions is unknowable, the questions themselves are invaluable. They allow us to move along a path of knowing ourselves more fully.

New questions enable us to see the familiar in a new light. My questions regarding shame helped me reshape a long-simmering conflict that, like Wanda, I had not been able to put my finger on. The new questions served as the missing link.

One Christmas a few years before my sense of self started to unravel, I received a gift from my in-laws. It was a framed 8×10 picture of me and my spouse taken the prior summer, after we returned from a run.

I will never forget the words my mother-in-law said as she handed me the gift: "I found the best picture of you two."

I opened that package and instantly thought to myself, *Is this some kind of a joke?* The photo in question is one in which my spouse and I are standing next to one another. I almost do not know how to describe its most distinctive feature.

My eyes are closed. Let me be clear. I am not caught in a delightful moment with eyes clenched in slits of laughter. I am standing there full-on looking straight at the camera, only my eyes are shut. Wastebasket material.

I recall saying a little too ungraciously, "My eyes are closed."

My remark prompted my spouse to take the framed photo into his hands to get a better look. Then, he turned to me and said, "Lin, what do you mean? This is a great photo."

His words stop me in my tracks.

Emotions mobilize to keep us safe as we untangle ourselves from familiar expressions of who we are. This protective wiring can be problematic as it has the potential to send us on detours or arrest our forward progress altogether. We will learn to reframe these emotions, a crucial step in changing our response to disruption and one more step toward realizing the untapped potential resident within us all.

5

Transforming Ourselves

"How do I do this?" asks Irene, a fifty-two-year-old homemaker who had raised a large family.

Irene was one of a dozen women who gathered at an informal luncheon I hosted for those in or considering major change.

For Irene, the prospect of such a transformative journey, while interesting, felt out of reach. "I have a lot to lose," she says, looking from face to face around the table to see if anyone else understood. Irene was in good company. Those assembled were familiar with the consequences of risking stability in favor of a belief that there was something *more* for them.

This chapter will introduce *how* to move beyond resistance and give oxygen to *more*, especially amidst the responsibilities of our lives. We will begin the process of creating—then embracing—a newly reimagined self, one that is shaped by our growing connection to what holds value and meaning to us. We will reframe the emotions that can mobilize to keep us in place. Through the process, we will learn how to live in alignment with our voices: differently, boldly, freer, and more enlivened.

By pursuing a transformational path, we discover how to greet the world differently. This path is available to all who accept the invitation of disruption. It is on this path that we learn how to bring our light and shine without even trying.

TOWARD A NEW SELF-DEFINITION

Transformation invites us to turn innovation toward our sense of self and develop a new self-concept. I created a toolkit called the "Incubator" to support us as we navigate such terrain. The Incubator is composed of four separate tools that function as a system to not only foster innovation in our self-concept but also support us through our emotional response to changes in our self-definition. The four are Resetting Expectations, Reimagining Identity, Reconstituting Connections, and Reframing Emotions. We use the latter to reframe our emotional response to personal transformation by using the letters of the word HAIL, Honor, Ask, Influence, and Learn, as activity prompts. Together, the tools of the Incubator enable us move beyond emotional resistance and grow.

I have worked extensively with the Incubator over the past five years, first in group settings with individuals who were working through transformation and later with attendees at workshops and speaking engagements. The tools can be used in any order. The order introduced in the upcoming chapters reflects the sequence preferred by those with whom I've interacted. I find that many individuals work through the initial few tools, then circle back to revisit one or another. The toolkit is flexible and designed to work with your needs.

For those with some clarity about what might be next, the Incubator helps you move further along with purpose, vitality, and newfound energy. For those with little or no idea about what might be next, the Incubator helps bring clarity, energy, and optimism to your journey. Through it, we learn to not only nourish our voices but also unlock the incredible potential resident in us all.

The Incubator is fashioned on a workhorse of the innovation economy: the start-up incubator. This renowned business model is a mini ecosystem that does everything in its power to ensure the success of its participant founders and their start-up companies. Since the late 1990s, hundreds of start-up incubators, like the now famous Y Combinator that fueled Dropbox, Airbnb, and Instacart, have popped up around the world.[1] When invited to join an incubator, a start-up company gains access to the people, resources, and know-how to help it succeed. While that in and of itself is impressive, an incubator's secret sauce lies in its ability to serve as a sandbox within which founders envision, test, and bring their dreams to life. My goal is the same for each of us through our Incubator.

A PREDICTABLE PATTERN

Our Incubator supports us as our self-concept progresses through a predictable set of growth-related activities. These activities are highlighted in the illustration that follows (Figure 5.1).

Let's use my story as an example of these actions. I began my journey by *re-examining* my assumptions about my work identity when I left Iron Mountain after "borrowing a car" and experiencing an escalating set of stressful disruptions. I *reframed* emotions like shame, self-doubt, and isolation that had mobilized once I began moving away from familiar expressions of who I was. I *revitalized* my beliefs about what

---

'How To' Transform Ourselves

* We **re-examine** beliefs, values, and expectations that constitute all or part of who we are.

* We **reframe** emotions that can mobilize to keep us in place.

* We **revitalize and/or create** new beliefs, values, and expectations for ourselves.

* We **disengage** from values, beliefs, and expectations that no longer serve us.

* We **integrate** these new and refined expectations, values, and beliefs into a new self-concept.

* We **act** in accordance with this new self-concept.

Figure 5.1. "How To" Transform Ourselves.

work could or should be, a step that led me to embrace the new roles of author, speaker, and researcher. I *disengaged* from prior expectations about what it meant to be successful. I started to *integrate* my updated personal expectations into a new self-definition, one that made room for more of my own voice in my work. I learned to *act* in accordance with these newly defined self-concepts—for myself and in the presence of others—and with my voice's newfound strength.

Taken together, these steps translate into something magical; they create for us a deeper connection to our own truth and build momentum that has the potential to alter the trajectory of our lives.

A CASE STUDY IN TRANSFORMING ONESELF

Lakshmi underwent a radical transformation of who she was. "I loved the connections these tools helped me make. I am in a different place because of this work," says Lakshmi, a thirty-two-year-old woman from Winnetka, Illinois. She served for years as a tester of the Incubator's tools and joined me for coffee to update me on her progress.

Lakshmi's journey began when she was a student in a rigorous MD/PhD program at a Big Ten university. "After the first year of the program, I realized, *This is not who I want to be.* The realization was crushing and chaotic." This awareness prompted Lakshmi to begin a process whose destination was unknown.

Lakshmi's family immigrated to the United States from Paris when she was ten. She and her four brothers were always pushed to achieve academically. They lived in a meticulously kept walk-up apartment near the Massachusetts Institute of Technology (MIT), a world-renowned university where her mom and dad were both academic researchers in the field of molecular biology.

She told me a story about her family's intractable beliefs about who she was. "One weekend I invited my graduate school roommate to join me for a few relaxing days at my parents' house in Cambridge. We were ready to explore the city, a place my roommate had never visited," starts Lakshmi.

"To my surprise, we walked in the back door to find the Taulks, family friends, waiting for us with my parents. My mother invited them to join us for dinner so I could tell them in person about my exciting MD/PhD program. She had put out her *best* china," says Lakshmi with an air of resignation in her voice.

THE EXPECTATIONS WE CARRY

"I was always 'the me' that I saw when I looked through other people's perceptions of me," Lakshmi says as I ask her about the expectations she carries for herself.

"I thought that my attractiveness to other people was about being smart. So those were the environments I was in and that is what got responded to. I always assumed that that's what I had to offer. If I didn't want to offer that, then who am I?

"I didn't know what to do," she says flatly. "I was aware that if I do not want academic medicine, who am I? I was feeling very confused and very lost without the perception of 'me' I always held."

Awareness is a critical first step as we make our way along a path of growth. As part of this journey, we raise our awareness of who we are and the values and beliefs that are active for us. We also use awareness to bring new thinking to assumptions we hold about ourselves and our roles, acknowledging that there are often many roles we occupy. We use awareness again to consider which of those expectations, if any, have outlived their useful lives.

"I was working sixty-to-seventy-hour weeks. It was exciting. But after a certain while, it stopped being meaningful," offers Lakshmi. Her realization did not translate into an instant answer. "The adrenaline continued to be a stimulant." She takes a breath, as if forgiving herself. "I was slow to realize that if I get an MD/PhD, I will be qualified to teach and do research in a university, which meant I would be living my life in the same environment that's crushing me right now.

"I did not know what to do," says Lakshmi of her growing awareness. "I never even dreamed outside of that world."

NAVIGATING EMOTIONS

Our emotions mobilize to keep us safe at times of upheaval in our identity. "I was in pain," shares Lakshmi when I ask about how it feels to be in this place. "And lost. It was chaotic and lonely. I was sort of marooned, totally isolated from myself and from my familiar community whom I could talk to," she says.

I was curious about her reference to isolation. It was a sentiment I heard from many others in my research. I venture to ask her, "Why did you feel isolated?"

"I didn't know what I would say," she starts. "There was a kind of confluence that created silence. Part of the confluence was that I didn't know what I was going through. I knew that I had to stop working in academic medicine, but I didn't know where I would wind up. With my closest friends, I could babble, and they could be encouraging but little else. I was very alone.

"I reached the point where I started having kind of early warning physical health symptoms: *headaches*. I ignored them for a while," she says and then continues, "My pain became debilitating. It was excruciating at the time and extremely upsetting."

Lakshmi's growing awareness helped her reframe her pain. "It really helped me connect more to my curiosity. I kept asking myself, *What is it that I have to figure out that my body is telling me that my mind does not get to know yet?*"

STEPS TOWARD A NEW SELF-CONCEPT

Lakshmi investigated taking a leave of absence from her graduate program as an initial step. "The hardest aspect of that transition was actually taking the first step, which for me was taking a leave of absence. It was the first step on kind of a radical renovation of self. Up until that time, *I* knew myself through the gaze of others.

"Taking a leave of absence was even more momentous than it sounds because it was really the first time I asked myself what do *I* want to do, and who do *I* want to be. The leave of absence began a massively transformative journey."

Lakshmi's work on re-examining her assumptions led her to a new level of understanding of herself and how she operated in line with her identity. "Once I made the decision to take the leave of absence, things changed," continues Lakshmi buoyantly. "It was adventurous. I was never afraid of wandering." She takes a breath and smiles, adding, "Once I let myself go there, it was letting go of so much. I knew what it meant. I needed to rebuild my internal architecture.

"And then, you know, I changed. I realized, *This is not who I want to be*. It was scary and demanding. I volunteered for AmeriCorps and got myself into community health outside of the classroom." She pauses for a moment, recalling this crucial step.

"This step helped me confirm the right direction to be moving in. So that kind of became the pattern. It was not necessarily knowing what my next phase would be but becoming confident that I would figure it out and that things would appear that would help me figure it out. This pattern helped me be more proactive and, over time, head in a direction I would never have imagined for myself."

These steps are ones we all go through as we reimagine our self-definition. A series of small steps combine to inform our new thinking about who we are.

"I found myself more and more interested in individuals, then families, and then their community. I was working with Latin refugees. I speak Spanish, and I became a founding member of a group that coordinated care and services for Spanish-speaking families. That got me interested in larger systems, and that led to systems thinking in organizations. The pattern helped me know what my next steps could be.

"I learned something important in all of this," she offers. "As odd as it seems, negative self-talk, shame, and perfectionism drove me to succeed for many years. Yet, it was a success I never really thought I was a part of. It continually needed to be refilled." Lakshmi, like all who progress along this path, built the capacity to meet this new knowledge with compassion. The Incubator's process creates the space to welcome past behaviors without judgment. In our work, past behaviors can add wisdom and perspective to the choices ahead.

NEW CONNECTIONS

The steps Lakshmi took proved beneficial on many levels. They helped her make new connections with others, which, in turn, deepened her understanding of herself. "I worked at a technology company on organizational behavior," says Lakshmi of a summer internship she landed at a joint venture between the University of Chicago and local technology start-ups. "It was big and a total surprise. I loved the work. It was thrilling, and it helped me move further into knowing *me* in new ways." She pauses and adds, "And I could do it. That I could do it," Lakshmi finishes, "*That* was startling."

"I realized something through the internship and the new job. It's kind of a big deal," says Lakshmi tentatively. "People liked me, they just liked me. I did not have to quote anybody. They just liked me. This was mind blowing to me."

Lakshmi met success as she acted in alignment with her new self-concepts. And she was affirmed by those around her. She adds, "And two other things I learned about myself. One is that I am funny, and two is that I am looked at as a leader. That was just *startling*."

Lakshmi's experience illustrates one of the most powerful findings from my research. In growth, we meet ourselves through our connections with others. Lakshmi offers, "They listened, really listened to me, and called me *insightful*." She still seems amazed by this turn of events. "They helped me work through this newly enriched part of me that I was discovering. It was momentous."

AN ENRICHING PROCESS

Transformation gently guides us to something more, a greater sense of who we are. When I ask Lakshmi about this deeper connection to the self, she offers, "I saw a more sincere and exquisite part of myself." Lakshmi takes a breath and adds with surprise in her voice, "This journey was such a *whopper*. It was like a massive identity shift.

"The tools gave me the confidence that I could survive the process and that—no matter what—something good would come out of it.

Having gone through that and not just survived, but thrived, gives me a new confidence to take on future disruptions.

"I think the vocabulary—the very fact of there being vocabulary—means that the experience somehow holds a higher authorization. It is an indication that there has been credibility given to the experience. I cannot overstate how positive this was for me.

"Growth is not the fantasy you hoped for where you just say to the world, 'Look, I want to do this,' and a big opportunity welcomes you with open arms. You have to work at it, starting with baby steps that give you an experience base, and then a résumé, that will then enable you to get to that fantasy."

I ask Lakshmi to describe the outcome of her process, expecting to hear about her new job or career. "I finally got to a place where I accepted not knowing. I would *never* have imagined that I could be in this place after where I started."

Transformational growth invites us to live in closer proximity to who we are at our essence. It is a process of coming into our own voice. The Incubator supports us as we discover and learn to live in alignment with this updated expression of ourselves.

THREE HIGHLIGHTS FROM LAKSHMI'S JOURNEY

Lakshmi's inspirational story highlights three elements of our Incubator's secret sauce: a reliance on *awareness techniques*, a bias toward *informed experimentation*, and a willingness to continually refresh the *questions* that guide our journey. With these, we can, like Lakshmi, realize the enormous upside from growth.

Awareness techniques lie at the heart of the Incubator. For our purposes, "awareness" means "coming into knowing." For example, Lakshmi became *aware* of gaps between her own thinking about who she was and the beliefs of those around her. This type of awareness plays a critical role throughout all stages of our work together and is combined with journaling prompts throughout the Incubator to support your progress.

I realize that the term "awareness technique" may be unfamiliar to you, but I would venture to guess that you are familiar with what it represents. For example, you have been introduced to an awareness technique if you have ever taken a yoga class. Yoga instructors typically begin classes by leading students through an awareness technique during which students are guided to notice the entry and exit of their breath into and out of their bodies. Without any other direction, participants inhabit their bodies differently thanks to being aware of the breath's presence and activity. Awareness techniques, for our purposes, accomplish something similar. They help bring a fresh perspective to something that may be right in front of us. The Reflections used throughout the Incubator are great examples of such techniques.

Informed experimentation is a supportive approach that is baked into "how" we make progress in defining a new self-concept. Informed experimentation requires that every time we act, we do so in such a way as to take the next *smallest* step—nothing more—in a direction informed by our questions. Lakshmi's reinvention did not happen in one step, as if she left academic medicine one day and landed a coveted organizational development internship the next. There were several steps in between.

Each step was informed by Lakshmi's interests as best as she could define them at the time. Her many steps started with a leave of absence, followed by volunteering with AmeriCorps, joining local community groups, observing others' behaviors in her new activities, engaging with others in a conversation about what she observed, starting a new organization to serve the needs of the community, and working with individual recipients and local partners whose usage patterns helped her notice behavioral similarities. Only after these many next smallest steps was Lakshmi ready to apply for the internship.

The Incubator anticipates a progression like Lakshmi's. It never endorses swinging for the fences or risking our entire existence with a single decision. Instead, the Incubator asks that we grow by taking one and then another next smallest step. For one person, the next smallest step might be listening to a podcast on a Tuesday at 10 p.m. after the kids are finally in bed. For another, the action may be interning without pay on an organic farm in New Zealand for six months. The specifics of any one step are less important than our willingness to take one and then another. In transformational growth, we repeat this pattern again and again in an iterative fashion until such time as continual small steps become a new behavior. This new behavior propels us forward.

Finally, our ability to use the Incubator to create a new self-definition relies on our willingness to ask ourselves *questions*. Questions invite us to clarify and refine the scope of that which we are willing to address. Lakshmi started out by asking, "Who am I outside of academic medicine?" and progressed to asking, "What might be possible for me as a leader in the field of organizational development, a funny and inspiring one at that?"

Our questions are never static as we progress along the path of growth. Every small step we take allows us to see ourselves and the world through a new pair of lenses, similar to Chapter 3's discussion of transformational growth. Lakshmi's questions helped her reformulate the scope of her journey and walk in an iterative fashion toward its promise.

Questions influence our actions in profound ways. It is not because they produce the perfect answer. What questions create is even more useful than answers; they initiate valuable new lines of questioning that serve as on-ramps to our understanding more and more of who we are.

These three elements, including a reliance on *awareness techniques*, a bias toward *informed experimentation*, and a willingness to repeatedly refresh our *questions*, sharpen our understanding of our journey and advance us along a path that is required for us to be successful on our own terms. This path is available to anyone willing to choose growth in the face of a gateway disruption.

◆

A REFLECTION: YOUR QUESTIONS

What is your journey all about? Is yours about moving to a new city, revitalizing a special relationship, resuscitating a career, or addressing something that does not feel quite right? The following exercise centers on your experience and starts our work with the Incubator.

Step 1: What is your growth journey about? Please feel free to write a journal entry, draw a picture, make a collage, write a poem, or create a bulleted list for your answer. Please choose whatever format works best for you.

Note, what comes to mind for many people in answer to this question stems from their experience of disruption. You may want to refer to the "Disruption and You" Reflection in Chapter 1.

Step 2: Try writing or rewriting your answer to Step 1 in the form of a *question*.

For example, Lakshmi might ask, "How will I define myself outside of academic medicine?" Someone grappling with a crossroads in a relationship might ask, "Who am I without my former significant other in my life?"

Step 3: What emotions come to mind as you ask the question from Step 2?

Step 4: What would you do if you were tasked with taking one small step in the direction of answering the above question?

For example, Lakshmi might say, "I will investigate what it means to take a leave of absence from my program."

REFLECTION-IN-ACTION

Heather, forty-one and an account executive at a prestigious advertising firm in New York City, asks herself a straightforward question: "What work can I do that will *mean more* to me?" In the same breath, she adds, "I am at a crossroads. I am not sure if I have the stomach to start over at this point in my career.

"When I got pregnant with my second daughter, my boss had some reservations about my ability to handle the job with two children at home. I was totally committed," she offers emphatically. "The distrust from my boss led to so much stress and pressure. I felt like I was walking on eggshells every day at work."

Heather's attempt at balance between work and family translated into an endless stream of upheaval. She notes, "The pressure was intense. I was not surprised when my job was affected by a reorganization. Our largest account, a nutritional supplements line, withdrew their business from our firm. I lost my job as a result." She adds, "I was both upset and kind of happy. It was a struggle every day going to work."

While the job loss was concerning, Heather looked at it as an opening. "I am thinking a lot about how *there needs to be more* when I get to the office. As a working mom—with the drop-offs, the babysitter switches, and all the outsourcing you do as a parent of young kids—my job needs to mean more than selling another power bar."

Heather had been an athlete all through high school and college. Early on, the work really appealed to her own focus on nutrition and well-being. She had less and less time for that world with her growing family. Without that ballast, she did not know which way to turn. "I don't know. I know I need another job. It's so hard. Going in another direction at this point feels like a restart. Not sure I am up for that."

Her next small step was research. "I need to think about meaning and the work I like." She finishes by saying, "I am terrified," and then adds, "And hopeful."

❖

DISCOVERING MORE

Questions repeatedly shift throughout a transformational journey. Their dynamic—not static—nature is an integral part of our ability to define a new self-concept. We have nothing to fear about questions that evolve. We should, in fact, cheer when one question opens up another.

The question at my own journey's outset focused entirely on work. What *job could I do* that would let me be more of the parent and professional I envisioned? As I continued to unravel after my work/family crisis—when my babysitter was on the verge of quitting after I "borrowed a car" on the way home from work—I was certain that switching my job would address whatever was occurring for me.

As my transformational path progressed, my questions changed. Thanks to consistent small steps, I found new work—as an author, speaker, and researcher on adult transitions. While I loved this work, my growth process continued. My questions reflected the ongoing nature of that progression and led me to understand a broader focus for my journey.

I am acutely reminded of this fact one day while on another stage sharing my newfound passion for adult growth. It is two years after the New York City event where I questioned my "right" to be an author. Now, I am invited as the keynote speaker for the Women's Leadership Conference in Oklahoma City. My job this morning is enormous. I need to create the energy in the room for a thousand attendees who are there for a day of inspiration and self-discovery.

I am on the stage looking out at the audience, all of whom are working on an exercise together. Admittedly, the exercise is a risky move. I recall having to convince the conference's director that I could pull it off without losing control. "No worries," I remember saying to her. An "exercise" in this environment meant that I had to coordinate one thousand people getting up, working with someone new to them, and sitting back down again, all within a matter of minutes. This did not frighten me. I am well versed in creating an atmosphere that turns a large-format speech into something that feels like a chat with a friend over the kitchen table.

The audience loves this opportunity to connect with one another. Everywhere I look, people chat animatedly, as if they found a new best friend. From where I stand onstage, the sound of all those conversations is striking, a happy roar.

Yet, as I stand there looking out at them, I am struck by how alone I feel. *How odd*, I say to myself.

I am not in it.

I am outside of these new connections. It seems as if I am looking at the audience through a carnival mirror that is making the space between us comically distorted.

I do not have the luxury of staying with this thought. I drop back into speaker mode to finish the hour.

At the end of the speech, I make my way from the stage and run into the conference's director. "Wow! That was fantastic. You created such energy in the room! No one was on their phones," she says, pumping my hand in delight, grateful. I say relatively little. I am spent. I left every ounce of energy I had on that stage.

By the time I make it to the taxi stand, I am revived enough to wonder about what happened up there.

How could I feel so alone in a sea of people?

I am well practiced with the Incubator's steps. I walk through them instinctively. Once I get myself into a cab and begin the thirty-minute ride to the airport, the questions come easily. As I look out the taxi's window, the city falls from view.

What does alone *have to do with me? Why there? Why on that stage?* The feeling of alone feels strangely familiar.

Answers to the questions do not immediately come to mind. This does not throw me. I am tired, after all. I also know enough of the toolkit not to give up. I ask myself more questions.

"When am I *alone?*" I find it ironic that I ask this question while recalling that I was on a stage in a room jammed with people. Beyond that space, I know that as a mom with a full-time job in a busy household, alone in a *physical* sense rarely happens.

Could this feeling of alone mean something else?

I was there, but not in it. I know for sure I was seen by every person in that audience. They met a vibrant and energetic me on that stage. Yet, I struggle to reconcile this fact with how I felt: I was *there* on that stage but somehow separate.

Where else is this true? I wonder.

What about in my relationships with those closest to me? That question pops into my head unexpectedly. It pivots me in a direction I had cordoned off thus far in my journey.

I sink further into the cracked, maroon vinyl of the taxi's backseat.

All of my steps up to this point have focused on work or work-related themes. These were big, demanding, and proved immensely gratifying. But they were not *this*.

As the taxi pulls up to the curb at the airport's departures gates, I know. I have looked everywhere else. It is time to ask about my *feeling alone* in the relationships with those closest to me.

EMBARKING ON A JOURNEY

The chapters that follow, Chapters 6 through 9, offer deeper dives into each of the Incubator's four tools. Through them, we will learn how to transform ourselves by working in four areas, including emotions, expectations, narratives, and connections.

Throughout you will find vital techniques—Reflections and Check Steps—that will help you access your untapped capacity and activate more of the fullness of who you are.

III

EMBARKING ON YOUR JOURNEY

6

The Incubator: Reframing Emotions

It is only fitting to start the Incubator with our work on emotions, given their active companionship with us all along the path of growth.

Eric, thirty-seven, knew this. He chose to stay home full time with his two young children after a layoff left him without a job. "My husband, David, and I talked. We agreed that this would be a good decision. Longer term, this will be good. I want to go in a new direction when the kids are older.

"I never imagined it would be so difficult," he offers. "I was let go from my job. I wasn't particularly happy there. I was there for a long time. I stayed because of comfort and, you know, you build relationships. Now that I'm out of the job, I miss having work, but I don't miss the job. I went into accounting, to be honest, to understand how business worked. I kind of just went along with it. When I was let go, I asked myself, *Is this what I really want to do the rest of my life?* I'd rather be working outdoors than sitting behind a desk."

Even with a supportive spouse, Eric's shift in his identity mobilized a continuous wave of emotions. "To be honest, I am more anxious and depressed than I expected. Part of me is relieved to be out of that job." He pauses and adds, "I am conflicted."

He rattles off questions that play continuously in his head. "*Should I be doing this?* Who am I *outside of being Bobbie's and Brittany's dad?*

Don't get me wrong. We are lucky to be able to do this. But this is no picnic. No one tells you that you lose your identity once you step out of the work world. What was I thinking?"

Eric was also surprised by the reaction of his former colleagues. "My co-workers act like I never existed. I feel like I'm grieving the loss of someone. It's weird. I saw these people every day for ten years, and now they're gone. It is like I never existed to them.

"I go through ups and downs. My anxiety is all about not feeling like I am in control. I never imagined this would be so hard."

Eric describes a normal emotional response that occurs when we disengage from a familiar expression of who we are. This chapter will focus on how to reframe the emotions we encounter at such times. We can rely on these practical techniques to help us continue to progress along a path of growth while in the presence of oppositional emotions.

EMOTIONS AND SHIFTS IN IDENTITY

Eric's emotional response brought him face to face with anxiety and depression. Lakshmi, who disengaged from an academic medicine MD/PhD program as discussed in the last chapter, had an emotional response that was adventurous and momentous at times but, more often than not, was painful, chaotic, confusing, lonely, and isolating. The Incubator addresses these types of emotional responses to growth with its first and most essential tool: HAIL. This tool teaches us to reframe the emotions that mobilize to keep us in place during growth.

HAIL, a mnemonic, invites us to _Honor_ our emotional response, _Ask_ ourselves about it, consider its _Influence_ on us, and wonder what we might _Learn_ from its presence. These four steps work on many levels to shift the power away from an emotion's hold over us. Through it, we reframe our relationship with an emotion and infuse that relationship with new meaning.

"Reframing" is a word that is widely used but merits a quick discussion. Imagine I asked you to draw a picture of an elephant as if it were standing three feet away from you. Next, imagine that I asked you to draw that same elephant, only this time, imagine I asked you to do so from a hot air balloon floating high above the Serengeti. How you see that same elephant from these two vantage points differs. This is reframing. HAIL enables us to take something familiar, like a relationship with anxiety, and see it through a new lens.

By using the tool HAIL, we also understand our agency, or ownership, in relation to an emotion in a new way. Agency empowers us to act on our own behalf. The tool teaches us to take a critical extraordinary step: to neutralize an emotion's power *over* us.

HAIL has been extensively tested and found to be very reliable in reframing emotions. I based it upon best practices from psychology, neuroscience, biology, Eastern religions, yoga, and psychiatry.

The tool works to create distance between ourselves and our emotions. Through it, we learn that an emotion, like anxiety, is not a trait but instead a transitory, impermanent state. I think of this shift in a visual sense. For example, before I learned HAIL, I felt as if I was hanging on at the end of a rope controlled by an emotion, like sadness. It had the power to flail me around, this way and that. Sometimes, I barely held on. Try as I might to counteract it, sadness ran the show when it was active.

After I learned HAIL, I still experienced sadness, but I could place its influence outside of me. It was as if I could drop that same rope onto the ground next to me. Once on the ground, sadness lost its power over me. I was no longer susceptible to sadness changing directions on me willy-nilly. Once I achieved this step, I could then ask myself questions about sadness. Why is it active? What might its presence mean? And what might I learn from it? Through these steps, HAIL shifts the power away from sadness and back toward me.

The upcoming sections will introduce HAILing. The four steps— Honor, Ask, Influence, and Learn—are each described separately. Through HAIL, we learn to greet emotions differently and ready ourselves to initiate the Incubator's exciting tasks of reimagining our self-definition.

HAIL'S HONOR

HAIL's Honor invites us to name the emotions present for us and to notice how we bestow additional meaning onto those emotions.

"Embarrassment, fear, shame, a paralyzing anxiety, and isolation," says Talia, leaning toward the group, as if relieved to be talking about what she experienced. She continues, "I have a lot of expertise in pharmaceutical drug development. I feel like an old dog kicked to the curb." A lot of heads nod around the table as Talia shares how it felt to lose her job. "I feel vulnerable, raw. One day, you know, 'I got it all going on,' and the next day, I don't." She takes a long breath and adds with a sigh, "I feel estranged from my colleagues with whom I am very close." After thinking a moment, Talia looks around the table and says, "I do not feel safe. I am scared. Financially, this is very frightening." She pauses and adds, "I hate the feeling of not being needed."

Talia Honored her emotions by naming those present for her and refraining from ascribing additional meaning to them. By Honoring, we validate the emotions by giving voice to the emotions we are experiencing. We say them out loud. *Anxiety. Fear. Shame. Guilt. Regret. Isolation. Relief. Joy.* We name them in all their forms. This step alone is valuable and helps us validate our experience of the emotions; we lend credence to their presence. Naming elevates emotions and helps us recognize them as worthy of space and time.

Honoring asks that we take one more step. We notice how we reflexively assign additional meaning to our emotions. For example, we notice when we say, "I am so anxious," and then add, "There must be something wrong with me." Honor asks that we name anxiety and notice as we attempt to layer on additional meaning to the emotion's presence.

Think about it. Regret? *Good morning.* Self-doubt? *Hello.* Anxiety. *Welcome back!* For example, if we welcome back sadness, Honor asks us to *notice* our desire to reflexively assign meaning and, for the time being, *refrain* from doing so. This request asks us to hold off applying meaning, as in, "I am such a failure!"

Honoring simply asks us to raise our awareness of that which is present for us and notice the reflexive practice of assigning additional meaning to that presence. I might feel anger or shame. Without thinking, I might *also* assign additional meaning to it with, "There must be something wrong with me." Honoring asks us to become aware of that reflexive bestowing of additional meaning and simply focus on validating the presence of emotions.

Honoring is countercultural. It does not require us to respond in any way. We name what is present. Full stop. The shame. The feeling of being overwhelmed. The failure. The hope. The curiosity. The relief. The heartbreak. The fear. The optimism. The anger. The inferiority. The joy. It all offers us important insights into what is walking with us as we make our way through transformation.

HAIL'S ASK

HAIL's Ask invites us to turn our curiosity toward the emotion and consider its meaning in our experience. Amie, a fifty-five-year-old empty nester, says, "I was prepared for the loneliness. I never imagined how difficult it would be to get back into the workforce. I shouldn't even bother. I am not qualified for any job." She talked at length with me about feeling lonely after her youngest moved out of the family home. Amie described herself as a professional volunteer who was extremely active in her church. She had been out of the conventional workforce for decades. "I am afraid. I do not feel in control. I do not think I can stomach failure," she starts. "Why bother?" she adds haltingly. Amie Honored her emotions by listing loneliness, fear, lack of control, an inability to concentrate, and self-doubt.

The Ask step invited Amie to explore the meaning of what was showing up for her. Why these emotions? What might they mean? These questions revealed some powerful linkages. "I cannot help but compare myself to others," she continues. "Many of my neighbors have always worked while raising their families. I've been out [of work] so long." Amie pauses a second and adds, "I never really felt successful when I was working. The job was a job. I struggled with confidence even then. What was I qualified to do?"

Asking begins to create more distance between ourselves and the emotion. Why might this emotion be showing up, and why now? When did it arrive? How long is it planning to stay? Asking helps us recognize something else very important. We are not the emotion; the emotion is the emotion. Amie's self-doubt is an emotion, not a trait of hers. Asking compels us to observe the emotion as something outside of ourselves that is temporary.

Amie observes, "My confidence suffered in the workplace, but I am generally a confident person." Her curiosity helps her go further. "I need to hold on to this feeling," she says with a broader smile. "Take *that* self-doubt!"

Asking helps us change the position of the emotion in relation to us. Joanne Cacciatore, an expert on grief, offered a powerful example of Asking in her book, *Bearing the Unbearable*. She said, "We are *feeling* heartbroken,"[1] which represents something very different from, "We are heartbroken." While only one word differs between these two statements, their meaning and power over us change radically if we are able to place the emotion outside of ourselves by recognizing it as temporary.

Asking compels us to think of ourselves as separate from the emotion. Through it, we begin a conversation with ourselves about where and how to place ourselves in relation to an emotion's presence.

HAIL'S INFLUENCE

HAIL's Influence invites us to bring our awareness to the emotion's role in our experience. Ayana, forty-two, worked for sixteen years at a well-known movie production company and learned about her spouse's intentions to leave their marriage on the day she returned from an extended international assignment. "I was so embarrassed. And panicked. We were married for seventeen years," she says.

Ayana and I were sitting in her kitchen near Huntington Beach, California, a place she had called home since her late teens. I asked her to consider the Influence of these emotions, like embarrassment.

"My identity was ripped from me." She pauses and looks out at the little garden just outside the window from where we are sitting. "I am not going to lie to you," she says. "The whole thing threw me into a crisis. I felt scared, rudderless, and vulnerable in ways that were complete and overwhelming." The Influence drove her to act in an uncharacteristic fashion. "I went into hiding so that I would not run into anyone I knew."

After the initial shock wore off, Ayana could see broader Influence stemming from this unexpected jolt. "*Who am I* without this marriage?" She adds in an urgent, sincere tone.

"This time went so much deeper than the earlier one. There were overlapping themes." Ayana recalls an earlier disruptive period: regaining her health and independence after an accident required a prolonged hospitalization and intensive recuperation. It was nearly two years before she got back to functioning as she always had.

She recalls asking a similar question of herself then, "*Who am I* without the recovery?" There were parallels between her two experiences. "This time is different from earlier. It struck my value system." She pauses and adds, "This last whopper of being kicked out of my marriage led to an amazing opening for me."

I smiled, grateful for her willingness to share this wonderful turn of events. "I would never have discovered this without the breakup of my marriage."

By considering an emotion's Influence, we broaden the scope of the information through which we experience it. The emotions do not magically disappear once we consider their Influence. Instead, Influence invites us to see emotions in a broader context. By considering them in this way, we interrupt an emotion's power over our thoughts, beliefs, and behaviors. We also gain visibility across our own circumstances, like Ayana's recognition that there were similarities between her recuperation and the breakup of her marriage. Most importantly, HAIL's Influence helps us ask new questions of ourselves.

HAIL'S LEARN

HAIL's Learn invites us to consider what the presence of an emotion might teach us. Rebecca smiled as I talked about Learning from her experience. "I always edit myself," says Rebecca, twenty-seven, as she describes filtering herself in many ways. This behavior seeped into the words she chose, how she comported herself, and even how she dressed.

Rebecca worked as an assistant curator at a world-renowned museum. She and I sat talking at a café table in New York City's Central Park, steps from the museum where she worked. A mutual friend introduced Rebecca to my work after her recent breakup with her significant other.

"I am so worried about just being too much. *Honesty* is my truth. I always worry about being *too* honest. I spend a lot of energy filtering me."

Even though she knew on one level the breakup was a good decision, she could not escape the emotions. "I am lonely, afraid, brokenhearted, and sad, so sad. We had a lot of fun together," she says, describing their six-year relationship.

"What might sadness be here to teach you?" I ask. She exhales a bit with this question as if our conversation offers her a much-needed welcome to talk freely about her feelings.

"Could my sadness be telling me to finally step away from perfection? I know I need to release myself from it. All the constant filtering, it is exhausting! Who knows? Maybe I am sad because I will not allow myself to be 'me'—*anywhere*. Do I even trust myself?" Rebecca looks surprised by what she just shared. She thinks for a second or two, shrugs her shoulders and says, "Oh well. With that said, I guess I should keep going."

"If I were more trusting of myself, maybe those around me would react more positively to me, my *honesty*." She offers, "It might be better for everyone."

Rebecca was quick to realize that her perfectionism had a range of influences. "This is not only about me and the people at work. It was a factor in Scott's and my breakup."

HAIL's Learning about our emotions often expresses itself as the polar opposite of our experience of the emotion itself, as in Rebecca's sadness inviting a release from the burden of perfectionism. Often, we arrive at such potential linkages by asking ourselves questions: What might the emotion represent for us? What do we notice about the conditions that are active when the emotion is present? If we are able to pivot and look at emotions from a new lens, they can offer us important clues relevant to our growth.

Few of us take the time to consider emotions in this way. Let's face it, if you had asked me what I might learn from my exhaustion as I felt disconnected from my work and "borrowed a car" on the way home from work one afternoon, I would have looked at you puzzled.

Many of us find it difficult to sit down and suddenly conjure a lesson from the presence of an emotion. Over the years, I have come to rely on a Buddhist meditation practice called "tonglen" for those, like me, who fall into this category.

Tonglen, in its purest form, is a meditative practice that uses the breath to focus on giving and receiving. On the "in-breath," practitioners think about the suffering, in any form, that they or others experience. On the "out-breath," practitioners focus on how to relieve that suffering in a universal way.

A modified tonglen can be used to support HAIL's Learning step. On your in-breath, consider an emotion, and on your out-breath, wonder about how to address that type of emotion in the world at large. For example, on my in-breath, I could focus on sadness, a consistent emotion that is a strong internal form of resistance for me. On my out-breath, I might focus on how to bring joy to the lives of those who experience sadness. This exercise helps me ask new questions of myself that can lead to a new understanding of sadness. This amended tonglen can support anyone for whom HAIL's Learning step feels out of reach.

◆

A REFLECTION: HAILING OURSELVES

Let us turn now to experimenting with HAIL by using it to address emotions in your own experience. This Reflection will walk you through each of HAIL's four steps.

> ***Step 1:*** Think about a time of growth in your life. Write down a headline to describe this experience. If you have not pursued a transformational path, feel free to use any time of major change in your life.
>
> *For example, Rebecca might write, "Releasing perfection's chokehold over me."*

Step 2: Honor
  Name the emotions active for you at the time of your headline. Notice when you apply meaning to the emotions, like, "There must be something wrong with me." Write down as many

emotions as come to mind. Also, feel free to jot down any expressions of meaning that you find yourself applying.

Step 3: Ask

Choose one emotion from the list you created. Ask yourself about that emotion. What might the presence of this emotion mean to you? Why is it active now? If you are stuck, try responding to the following prompts:

Hi [fill in the emotion, e.g., anxiety].
Why are you here?
Why now?
What do you want to achieve on this visit?
When did you arrive?
How long are you planning to stay?
Did you bring anyone else along with you?
Is your visit today different from the last time I saw you?

Step 4: Influence

Write down how this emotion Influences you.

For example, if I listed my emotion as "sadness," I might write down that it Influences me by making me withdraw from others or feel weepy.

Step 5: Learn

Imagine that you can learn something from your emotion. What might you Learn from its presence?

For example, Ayana might list "vulnerable" as her emotion. She might learn that she has more strength in her ability to withstand the shock of her husband's announcement than she is willing to grant herself, similar to her earlier experience with recovery.

If you would like to try tonglen, follow the prompts below:

- Sit in a comfortable position where you can breathe in and out uninterrupted for a few minutes.
- Start by observing your breath entering and exiting your body.

- On your in-breath, focus your thoughts on your emotion, and on your out-breath, focus your thoughts on how you might address that type of emotion in the world at large.
- Repeat these steps for two to four minutes.
- Once complete, go back and answer the question in Step 5.

Step 6: Write your observations about using HAIL.

REFLECTION-IN-ACTION

Ashley, forty, was in a tough spot. She lived in Virginia Beach, Virginia, in a multi-generational household with her son, husband, and her husband's parents. She wanted to start a business from home doing communications for small companies. She had been toying with this idea for a long time. She saw it as a way to relieve some of the financial burden on her husband and a way to do something for herself. This was the type of work she had done prior to having her son. She had not worked outside of the home for twelve years.

To Honor her emotions, Ashley listed many of them, including exhaustion, self-doubt, isolation, stress, fear, and hope. "I am exhausted. I am emotionally drained. Most days I cannot even think about what's next because I have a thousand things to do," she says in a tone that reveals the weight of sustained exhaustion that is familiar to many of us regardless of our circumstances.

For Ask, Ashley decided to work with fear. It showed up for her when she thought about adding some part-time work to her other responsibilities. "By meeting my husband's needs, my child's needs, the household's needs, I lose myself." Fear held a lot of meaning for Ashley. She adds, "I *never* feel 100 percent successful. So, I am afraid. Can I really take on more?"

Ashley was easily able to see how her fear Influenced her. "I constantly worry about what other people think. I go, go, go all the time. I think women are taught to please others. So, I am embarrassed to say this, I still . . . I see myself led by a desire to please and get approval from others. It is exhausting! I cannot believe I still do this at forty."

HAIL's Learn prompted Ashley to consider herself and her needs in a new way. "I think fear is telling me to start listening to myself instead of waiting to hear what everyone else thinks." She pauses and adds, "It is hard to talk to the people you are closest to about starting a business because even though they love you and support you, they are judgmental because they have different mental models for how they think about things. Like your husband, if he has a different way of thinking than you do, even though he does not mean to discourage you, he may." Ashley knew instinctively that the answer for moving forward on her idea needed to come first from her own belief in it. "For this to even ever happen, first I have to start with a dream of it."

HAIL helped Ashley reframe her emotions and ask new questions about the importance of her own dreams.

❖

HAILING UNPLUGGED

HAIL can be a useful tool if used "in the moment" we are experiencing an emotion and if used "upon reflection" at some point after the emotion is active. I was thankful to be a HAIL power user recently because it helped me reframe an emotion in real time. Without HAIL, I would have stewed about this experience for longer than I would like to admit, a response that would have sapped my energy and led to all sorts of other work- and non-work-related stress.

Before the pandemic, I was awarded a consulting project to lead "talent" integration for a major acquisition at a large, publicly traded company. There were six other executives involved in the integration, many of whom I knew and had worked with in the past. Each of us had a single area of responsibility: sales and business development, operations, finance and administration, research and development, technology, and talent. One day, we held a day-long meeting with the company's CEO and CFO to review the plans and work through unresolved issues.

One executive, Peter, the technology (IT) lead, was antagonistic toward me throughout the project. This day was no exception.

Here is how the meeting unfolds.

Every time Peter speaks about an area, he references the lead person's name. For example, "Jack has more to do before IT can integrate the customer relationship management (CRM) system." Whenever he references the area of talent, my responsibility, he avoids naming me. He instead refers to "talent." "Talent feels uneven," or "Talent still needs to address that issue."

I am stunned by his behavior. I get angrier and angrier as the morning wears on. *How dare he?* I think to myself. Peter sits four feet away from me, but he avoids all eye contact. *How is that even possible?* I wonder. My anger notches up every time he opens his mouth. I am not someone who carries anger often, so anger feels raw and urgent.

We break for lunch. It is served in an adjacent conference room where there are high tables large enough for a person or two. I grab one of the deli sandwiches from the café cart and claim a table near the window. I open my laptop as if responding to an email, grateful for this decoy. I know I need to create space between myself and my anger. I use HAIL in hopes of reframing my anger before we reconvene after lunch.

This is how my internal conversation goes.

I Honor the emotions that come, including anger, disbelief, and self-doubt. What more can I say? I am hopping mad that he blatantly refuses to acknowledge my presence. He never once makes eye contact with me. Anger surprises me. I am not someone who gets angry often. Disbelief is knit together with anger. *How can this be happening?*

Self-doubt rolls in silently, like a fog. Try as I might to rise above this, anger pitches me off balance, leaving me vulnerable. While I am not sure it is an emotion, this fog separates me from the others. No one else sees it. Not the CEO, who is my longtime colleague and champion. Not the others. This feeling of separation fuels my self-doubt. Am I really seeing this? Am I making too much of his behavior?

I Ask myself about the anger. *Why was it showing up? Why here? Why now?* I instantly link Peter's behavior to disrespect. I bring orders of magnitude more experience than he does to the table. My anger is tied to his willingness to look through that. While interesting, I feel as if there is more to this.

HAIL's Ask invites me to stay with meaning and consider anger from additional angles. This second attempt is more potent.

I quickly bridge from feeling ignored to feeling unseen. This link appears contradictory; I am making critical contributions to the project, yet I am erased from the record in Peter's telling. By questioning the meaning of my anger, I discover this linkage to feeling unseen, a live wire for me. I can barely touch the thought without ricocheting off it. The feeling of being unseen troubles me to the core.

HAIL helps me get close to how anger Influences me over the course of the morning: I am distracted and lose track of the conversation, I withdraw from active participation, and I snap at Peter unnecessarily. This last one really breaks my heart. I was verbally curt with Peter. All that were present looked askance at me, surprised by the aggressive tone in *my* voice. It only happened once. Once was enough. I now look like the aggressor. Anger is powerful, distracting, and capable of thwarting the contributions I was hired to make.

Learning asks me to be bigger—and wiser—than my anger. What can I Learn from anger? I wonder whether it is tied to control somehow. *Am I upset because I cannot control what is happening or even control Peter's misbehavior?* That question does not feel right.

What comes up next is compassion, a state that, for me, occupies the opposite side of the spectrum from anger. *Are Peter or others around me in need of compassion?* I chuckle a little at this. While I am a magnanimous person, I am not sure I have a big enough heart to extend compassion in his direction after the morning I have had. Even so, I do not want to leave compassion.

What about compassion toward myself? If I start from this place, I see that, of course, I belong here, and I have made worthy contributions. Peter's baiting recedes from this place; I do not have to absorb someone else's behavior, particularly Peter's. Self-compassion feels important. The fog dissipates.

The tightness in my body releases. I breathe for a moment, more freely. HAIL helps me reframe my anger. Through its four steps, I am reminded that *I* matter. He does not set the stage for me. *I* get to decide how *I* show up.

The lunch break ends. I gather my things and go to my seat in the next room, my deli sandwich still uneaten. Peter takes up his seat across from me. I am unphased by his proximity. I am thoroughly engaged in the conversation for the remainder of the day. At one point, I pose a hypothetical question to the group that allows everyone there to bring more of their thinking into the conversation. I smile to myself as the meeting draws to a close, fully anchored in an entirely different place than I was only hours earlier.

As I make my way from the conference room, the CEO excuses himself from another conversation to come talk with me. "That was a terrific conversation. Thank you for being here."

Indeed.

◆

HAIL'S CHECK STEP

A "Check Step" is a short exercise designed to help you integrate the learning from this chapter into your own transformational journey. We will do one at the end of each of the Incubator's four chapters. Much like the Check Steps used broadly in the technology industry, these will prompt you to integrate your learning from this chapter into your plans.[2]

Growth invites us to notice outgrown self-concepts and create newly defined expressions of who we are. While this is an enlivening and joyful process, it also comes along with an emotional response to those changes. The Incubator's Reframing Emotions empowers us to revisit these emotions. Reframing not only helps us neutralize the emotion's desire to keep us in place but also positions the emotion to contribute information in support of our growth. Without HAIL, we could be mired in emotional resistance and never advance. With HAIL, we honor and learn from the presence of emotions and keep on going in the direction of our dreams.

CHECK STEP: HAILING OUR WHOLENESS

Step 1: What question guides your transformational journey? Note, you explored this same question in Chapter 5's Reflection, Step 2.

> *For example, Ashley's question might be, "What type of business can I start from home?" See this chapter's Reflection-in-Action for Ashley's story.*

Step 2: How has HAIL contributed to your thinking about growth? Write down what comes to mind. For a refresher, please refer to your answer to this chapter's Reflection, Step 6.

For those who would prefer prompts, spend a moment working through these questions:

- What emotions are active for you?
- What might the emotions mean in terms of your experience of disruption?
- How do your emotions influence you?
- Is there anything you might learn from these emotions?

Step 3: Revise the question from Step 1 that guides your growth journey by integrating your response from Step 2.

For example, Ashley might revise her question to be, "What changes do I need to make to believe in myself and my dreams?"

7

The Incubator:
Resetting Expectations

As we get comfortable reframing emotions, we can turn our attention to the work of recalibrating the assumptions upon which we architect our sense of self.

I recall vividly the conversation I had with Donna, a cancer survivor who was stymied in the aftermath of a divorce. "If not this, then what?" she asks, relating to work she had done on and off for decades and to her way of being. Donna grew up in a farming community in California's Central Valley. There she sharpened the traits that made her who she was. A hard worker. Loyal, with deep ties to family and those in her community. "I have been through so much," she says. "The cancer. Raising a family. Working, and not working. Why this time?" Donna asks rhetorically. She was angry and devastated over the failure of her marriage and surprised by how differently she felt in comparison to other disruptions earlier in her life. "I do not even know which way to turn."

This chapter begins our conversation on the role expectations play in our self-concept, like for Donna, who was stymied by shifts in her thinking. Here we will learn about the expectations we carry for ourselves and begin to get our arms around what it means to update them. We will also talk about "letting go" of expectations that may have outlived their useful life. Overall, we will work toward welcoming opportunities to reset the expectations that inform who we are.

WHAT ARE EXPECTATIONS?

The expectations we hold for ourselves are internalized beliefs that direct our thoughts and actions. They play a role in what we think, feel, and anticipate and how we behave. They serve as internal guardrails that help us determine if we are okay, safe, happy, successful, and loved. There are many expectations that we are aware of, like an expectation that we will be successful at our job. There are others that operate outside of our line of sight yet nonetheless actively influence our actions, as in beliefs we learned at a young age about how to treat other people. Expectations are automatic and part of the fabric of who we are. In most cases, we are not required to stop and think about when, where, or how to deploy them. That said, they are not absolute in their influence.

We learned in Chapter 3 that shifts in the values, beliefs, and expectations we hold for ourselves play an essential role in our journey through transformational growth. These shifts have come to life in the stories we have talked about thus far, like when Beth Anne confronted her beliefs about marriage in the wake of divorcing her husband. Or when Arthur shifted his understanding of what it meant to *see* other people.

Transformational growth is typically initiated in the aftermath of a gateway disruption, thanks to our awareness of a gap between long-held beliefs that conflict with our more recent experience. Our decision to address these gaps leads to the choice that stands as a foundational step in personal transformation.

SHIFTS IN OUR EXPECTATIONS

Expectations play a starring role in all stages of transformational growth. They are formed from a variety of inputs that differ depending upon where we are in our growth progression. Recall our discussion of these shifts in Chapter 3 in the section titled "The Illustration."

Prior to a transformation, the expectations we hold for ourselves are typically formed by a mash-up of influences that are external to us. These external influences can mirror those held by our families, the schools we attend, the occupations we choose, the communities in which we live, our religious affiliations, our racial or ethnic composition, our gender, and much more.

As we grow beyond this initial stage, our sense of self relies on broader expectations that are more self-defined and reveal more of that which holds value and meaning *to us*. These expectations reset as we grow, drawing us closer and closer to who we are at our essence, our truth.

If we continue to grow beyond a sense of self informed by self-defined expectations, we rely on additional inputs to reset expectations. These inputs supersede the individual and anchor our newly reset expectations on a transcendent interconnectedness with all else.

Our expectations, and the inputs upon which we rely to establish them, have the potential to continually shift throughout our lives.

EXPECTATIONS AND THE GROWTH PROCESS

The process of updating our expectations during growth can be uneven. In the movie version of growth, updating expectations is transactional: we leave one and turn to embrace another. In real life, however, expectation shifts occur in a less elegant manner.

As we progress through growth, the expectations we hold on any one day are a fusion of two types: those we have always occupied, and those we are advancing toward. Early on, the fusion tilts in favor of the past with only a glimpse at the future. Over time, we make room for more prominence of the new and greatly diminish the influence of the former. It is this shift that serves as the backdrop upon which we reset our sense of self. Participants in my research describe moving through such shifts as confusing, difficult, hopeful, and expansive.

Fatima, fifty-eight, a stay-at-home mom who struggled mightily with the prospect of an empty nest, described the difficulty of moving between long-established beliefs and those more closely aligned with her growing voice.

She and her husband were both attorneys. At thirty-nine, Fatima withdrew from the workplace after her youngest daughter was born with cerebral palsy. "It was difficult to be without a paycheck or a title or someplace to go for the first time in my adult life," she offers, recall-ing that period of time. "With all that went along with the demands of caring for our family, there was no time to think." Fatima's empty nest was being precipitated by their soon-to-be-departing daughter, who was moving into a new phase of independence.

Fatima pauses before continuing, "I am now for the first time asking myself the question, *What do I want to do?*" She found that answering this question was a lot harder than she anticipated.

"My daughter will soon move to an adult living residence," says Fatima. "Everyone is asking me if I am going back to practice the law. One day I want to get involved in developing more adult living environments for those whose capabilities are like my daughter's. We have far too few of these to meet the demand. Another day I am hav-ing lunch with my former colleague, a law partner, and we are talking about my joining his practice. I get excited."

Fatima used the term "ping-pong match" to illustrate how rapidly she toggled between her new ideas and her more conventional expec-tations. What she thought was the "right" answer constantly changed during this period of time. "I really have no desire to go back to law, but it is like a siren song. It keeps pulling me."

As we will see, the Incubator directs us to worry less about choosing the right answer and more about focusing on the beliefs and values that inform our expectations. By approaching a decision like Fatima's in this fashion, we achieve something especially important. We revisit and potentially reset layers of expectations that can shroud our desire to embark on a journey toward our newly expanding truth.

A CASE STUDY IN RESETTING EXPECTATIONS

Resetting Expectations is a continuous process that is ongoing even after we decide to move in a new direction. Pascal, who was in a place similar to Fatima, albeit for different reasons, knew this.

"Coming out was a process of going from exhaustion to relief," says Pascal, forty-three, who invited me for coffee on the porch of the brightly painted home he and his husband shared in the Bay Area. "The exhaustion for me was living up to expectations—this other life—that was not me, that was a total lie. The identity I was living, as a straight man, it was not who I was," says Pascal flatly.

"The exhaustion comes with keeping track of which story I told to whom. The deception and keeping track of the alternate narratives—stuff like that—stands in the way of honestly putting the pieces together. I was always dancing on the edge of being found out.

"I made sure that certain family members didn't meet certain friends because of my stories, stories that I created, but still, it wasn't who I was." He recalls one story that "I spun for the guys at home that me and this woman, a really good friend the first year [in college], had more of a relationship. Don't you know, she was visiting San Francisco over the holiday break. We ran into her at the Fillmore Theater—me and my high school friends. She was completely cool, acknowledged us with a smile and short hello. Then she went on with her friends. No one realized, but I was dying. I thought my ruse was over."

Pascal's words brought to light the many layers of disengaging from expectations tied to an established identity, however ill-fitting. "Awareness took a long time. I was aware of otherness tied to my being gay. I needed to almost prepare for acting on it. I was not ready to act on it for a long time. *Now's not the time*, I recall saying to myself over and over. Then, of course, I got to the point when I said to myself, *I am not going to deny this anymore.*"

Pascal's experience of becoming aware of miscast or outlived assumptions and a willingness to *act* on that awareness was a common thread in my research for all experiences of growth, regardless of an individual's circumstances.

"Coming out is about being ready. *I'm going to claim my true identity.* It was time for me to say, *Yes, this is who I am. This is me!*" In a sentence, Pascal perfectly summarized transformation for us all. Growth is about recognizing and coming to terms with who we are and then being willing to live in alignment with that truth.

This simple statement involves a number of resets. We become aware of the expectations we carry for ourselves, we refine those that fit, we disengage from or turn down the volume on those that are less relevant or outlived, and we reimagine new ones.

Resetting Expectations goes hand in hand with a decision about how much to let others see of ourselves. For Pascal, that meant coming out in a measured cascade, first to himself, then to his intimates, then to friends whom he deemed "ready" to hear such a message, and then to work colleagues and many others. "It is a very emotional issue for people. There are some communities where I am still not out entirely. It becomes more complicated when you are at various stages with different people."

I ask Pascal to describe how it felt to navigate this process of resetting the expectations that anchored his self-concept. "It is a safety issue. To step away from that identity, you feel so unsafe. You are either not going to be part of the family anymore; you are going to get kicked out, or you are going to to—*I don't know what*—these are real fears."

Pascal's fear is emblematic of what every one of us experiences as we contemplate disengaging from all or part of a stable, familiar, well-established identity.

We are not done once we become aware of and disengage from expectations that no longer fit. We are then tasked with establishing new expectations for ourselves, a process that itself is multi-layered.

Pascal continues, "There are many more layers of expectations because you've opened up a whole new world of identity that you never even knew once you step away from, in my case, the expectations tied to being straight. Then it was not about me passing as a straight man; it was about what it meant to be gay and part of the gay community." He pauses and, with a knowing smile, adds, "I took small steps. I cracked the door open a little bit. I first asked myself, *Am I in the right place?* And I waited to see some reactions before taking the next step." He knew this work was critical to resetting his expectations. "Over time, my small steps led the way to more clarity around the expectations that *now* serve as the foundation for who I am."

To his surprise, Pascal was very alone during this process. "The people that my family were making fun of, the flamboyant gay male, is not who I am. I needed to define for myself 'who I am' in this new world, outside of the assumptions others around me carried. Knowing that I needed to dispel their biases, while figuring this out for me, only made the process that much more isolating because my family could not share this with me."

Emotions mobilize in an attempt to keep us safe as we proceed in this manner. Pascal was not immune; his emotions fueled self-doubt.

"Did I make the right decision?" asks Pascal on the internal talk track that played on a continuous loop through this period. And then he adds, "I am not looking backward to the world I just left for validation. I am looking to this new, unfamiliar world, in my case, the big queer world, that I just stepped into, which is huge and as segmented as the other world I just left. I am testing, testing, to get a sense for where I fit in. It has been stressful and exciting at the same time."

Pascal's story highlights the progression of Resetting Expectations as we undertake transformational growth. At the outset, we focus on the challenging task of updating our relationship to our existing identifications. This involves raising our awareness of, refining and maintaining some, and getting rid of former identifications, including the ill-fitting ones that we hung on to for too long. Once we clear this stage, we find ourselves in an equally challenging place. Now we are working to make sense of ourselves in a different space, which in Pascal's case involved setting new expectations for himself as a gay man.

As we transform ourselves, we repeat this process again and again as we work through the composite of expectations that anchor our sense of self. We become aware of, refine, and potentially disconnect from former expectations and then begin the task of envisioning, shaping, testing, and living with the new expectations. This resetting is a normal growth cycle, one that invites us to ask broader questions of ourselves and gain a deeper understanding of who we are.

CRISSCROSSING POINTS OF REFERENCE

When we move away from long-held expectations, we invite instability for a time. To address this, we reflexively reach forward or backward to create some stability—if only temporarily. We often do so by embracing temporary, or provisional, expectations. Pascal relied on small tests as temporary expectations for a time as he gained better visibility into his new world.

In contrast to Pascal's approach, the vast majority of individuals in my research looked back to prior self-concepts for temporary stability. These individuals relied on previously held identity markers, a choice that added complexity and heartache to their desire to move forward.

Imagine you are a new teacher who has previously earned a living as a professional athlete. New to the teaching field, you might be in the throes of trying to figure out what success means. Without clear expectations, you rely on previous assumptions—like your prior earnings and the amount of time you exercise each day—in an attempt to establish some stability. The risk in this backward-looking approach is that you might feel like a failure early on because your new world of teaching pays you a much lower income and allows for far fewer workouts. Even though you made a conscious choice to enter teaching, these crisscrossed expectations leave you in an unsettled place, susceptible to emotions that can work against you.

Paulette, a nurse and naturalized Mexican American who spent all of her twenty-two-year career in Southern California, looked backward for provisional expectations as she grew. "I had decided to become an entrepreneur," says Paulette about a decision that would allow her to focus on helping families who had aging relatives in need of complex home care. She had really good reasons for going out on her own. She had worked for decades as a nurse manager and later the nursing supervisor for a local hospital. "I loved every minute, I loved working with my colleagues and the patients," she says enthusiastically and then switches to a more somber tone. "To be honest, it got harder and harder. I lost count of how many times the hospital reorganized." Staffing cuts came with every new organizational restructure. "I knew it was time," she says with conviction.

The early days of her business did not go as planned. "I mapped my old way of working onto the new business. I continued to operate as if success meant twelve-to-fourteen-hour workdays and being in touch with a large staff. I used these old beliefs and structures to measure myself." Even though she brought more than twenty years of experience to her work, she says, "I felt inadequate and ill-suited for my new role. So much so that I missed important deadlines for clients and scrambled to meet staffing needs."

This mapping of "old" expectations onto her "new" entrepreneurial venture proved problematic. Paulette offers, "I went through a period of denying my new self even after I made the decision to start this company."

Are you aware of reaching forward or back at times of growth? Awareness of this dynamic is part and parcel to our success. Once we are aware of the risk of crisscrossing expectations, we can learn how to operate differently. Paulette was emboldened by this newfound perspective.

"At first, I did not see that I was mapping old onto new. I felt like a failure. The old beliefs and structures carried over with me onto this new path. I suppose it was familiar, helping me be with the discomfort that went along with all of the *new*." Once she became aware of this behavior, Paulette was easily able to reframe her thinking and talk directly to her expectations. "Now, I say, *Ha, I see you!*"

Awareness of the expectations we carry for ourselves is a powerful enabling force in transformation. With it, we greet the expectations we carry for ourselves in a new way. We also learn that growth goes hand and hand with our willingness to re-examine the expectations that lie at the core of who we are.

◆

A REFLECTION: YOUR EXPECTATIONS

What expectations do you hold for yourself? Can you identify those that serve you well? Are there others that hold you back or work against your dreams? This Reflection begins your work in resetting the expectations active for you.

> ***Step 1:*** What expectations do you hold for yourself? If you are stuck, finish the prompts that follow.

These prompts may help you raise your awareness of your expectations:

1. I will be happy if . . .
2. I will be loved if . . .
3. I will be successful if . . .
4. I will be at peace if . . .
5. I will be relevant if . . .
6. I will be honest if . . .

7. I will be energized if . . .
8. I will be safe if . . .
9. I will have hope if . . .
10. I will be okay if . . .
11. I will have "made it" if . . .

Step 2: Are any of your expectations in flux or at risk of no longer serving you? Circle those on the list from Step 1 that fall into these categories.

Step 3: Take a moment to consider the values and beliefs associated with the expectations you hold most dear. Write down what comes to mind.

For example, Pascal's new expectations may include being a successful business leader in the gay community. He cites this expectation as an expansion of his beliefs about service and community that have been a part of his identity throughout his life.

REFLECTION-IN-ACTION

Emma, forty-two, a geologist who worked at a large southern university, quickly ticked off two expectations that were tied to her upheaval: her desire to have a family, and her thoughts about what a career should or should not be.

"I started with one dream. I always wanted to have a family. And then, I came to the sad realization that my number-one dream was not going to happen," she says calmly.

Emma married her college sweetheart and went to work at a university where her spouse was a faculty member. "I loved academia because my dad had taught at a small private college in the Midwest."

Emma got pregnant in her early thirties and was overjoyed to be beginning this phase of her life. Heartbreakingly, she miscarried at thirty-four weeks.

"One day you are pregnant," she says. "Then you are not. There is no baby. No one knows what to say." Her voice quivers. We both stop for a moment, taking in the gravity of her loss.

Emma and her spouse were devastated. While blanketed in grief, they were resolute in starting a family. Emma had difficulty getting pregnant a second time. She and her husband began what would be a difficult course of fertility treatments.

"Each pregnancy was so hard to come by. There was so much emotional upheaval for so long. My life kept starting and stopping in nine-month intervals." Emma pauses before continuing. "The doctors," she says, "they do not know. They tell you things, like reduce stress. They do not mean to, but it is hard not to internalize what they say. I blamed myself."

Emma quit her job in an effort to reduce stress. Thankfully, her colleagues helped her get a start on her own by asking her to do consulting projects in support of their research. After a year, Emma formalized this work by incorporating a new business.

"This was never in the cards for me. One day I felt liberated outside of academia, the next I felt terrified. I never thought of myself outside of that world. Starting a business? That was never something I was supposed to do."

One morning as she and her husband were getting ready for work, Emma called it quits on the fertility treatments. "That's enough. We are adopting." After seven treatment cycles and three more miscarriages, Emma was ready to disengage from her initial expectations about what it meant to parent and have a family.

"Once I made the choice to adopt, I never questioned again my assumptions about parenting. We love our daughter and our family life. On the entrepreneurial side, my expectations are still in flux. I find it really hard to imagine myself as a business owner even though I have been doing it now for years. I feel so uncertain as an entrepreneur. I am still operating outside of anything I know. This is hard."

◆

AWARENESS AND UNSEEN EXPECTATIONS

Reflections like this one can help us gain access to our expectations and the beliefs and values that underly them. We have talked about expectations that we are aware of, like Pascal's awareness of being gay, and others, like Emma's parenting desire early on, which are visible, deeply ingrained, and feel inflexible.

We have yet to talk about the expectations that are highly influential but less visible in our lived experience. These expectations are deeply established, even rooted in childhood, and often operate outside of our awareness. The Incubator can help us gain access to these expectations of which we may be unaware at the outset of our journey.

During my own journey, the Incubator increased my skill at using awareness techniques and helped me gain access to expectations of which I had been previously unaware. The new visibility helps me ask broader, more informed questions of myself.

When I was very young, I would guess seven or eight, I remember practicing for a neighborhood talent show. Several little girls from the neighborhood and I cooked up the idea for the show. The yard we chose for it was perfect. It had two picnic tables with long benches— essential for the throngs we anticipated.

I loved to sing and dance and perform, like other little girls across generations. On the afternoon of the show, I was twirling around in my bedroom, practicing my number. I wanted to get it just right. I chose a song from my coveted *Sound of Music* LP.[1] In 1971, that soundtrack was all the rage for young people my age. I played the record on my portable record player that sported a pink-and-blue flower-power design on its case. I practiced the number again and again to get my timing right. I sang at the top of my lungs. It was pure bliss.

"Turn that off!" came my mother's voice, explosive with anger. "What are you doing?" She screams as I turned to face my bedroom door, where she is standing perfectly framed.

"I am practicing for the talent show," I reply, confused but still holding on to my excitement.

"I have never been more embarrassed in my life," she says curtly. "Mrs. Cara and I were having tea out back." She was referring to the yard behind my childhood home where neighbors often gathered to catch up on the day's news.

She looks dismissively at the portable record player and me, standing on my homespun dancefloor—the space between the twin beds.

To this day, I am not entirely sure what embarrassed her. One thing I am sure of, I was forbidden to participate in the talent show. Instead, she forced me to watch my friends sing and dance from a lawn chair parked right next to hers, quite a distance from the makeshift stage and well behind the ready picnic table benches.

Being forbidden to participate that day is a form of shame I can easily connect to many other memories of my childhood. I can also connect it to an attitude of defiance I adopted early—maybe even at that moment while sitting in the neighbor's yard.

My awareness of this experience helps me ask new questions about the expectations I carry. Where is it okay to be me? What else in my behavior was I led to believe was embarrassing, inappropriate, or out of bounds?

Like so much of the Incubator's process, the accuracy of the answers to our questions is unknowable. That said, I hope to help you explore how the questions themselves, like my own about where it is okay to be me, are even more powerful than the answers.

At the start of my journey, I had not planned to explore where and under what conditions it was okay to be me. Yet, here I was, looking at this new question and believing in its right-mindedness.

Transformational growth is much less about a light-bulb moment and more about recognizing the expectations we carry, sometimes invisibly, and what may be holding us back. I may never know why my mother was embarrassed by me. I know I no longer wish to be regulated by its influence.

◆

A CHECK STEP FOR OUR EXPECTATIONS

Resetting Expectations increases our awareness of the expectations we carry and the sources upon which we draw to set those expectations.

With growth, we invite ourselves to update and refine the expectations we hold for ourselves, thereby expanding the inputs upon which we architect our sense of self. Resetting Expectations is a process that involves raising our awareness of the expectations we carry, recognizing which ones may no longer serve us, and establishing new expectations that can guide our exciting forward path. This cycle is repeated again and again as we move through transformation. In fact, most of the individuals in my research started their journey by focusing on one aspect of themselves and then began re-examining more and more of the layers of expectations that together form their self-definition. In the chapter that follows, we begin the conversation about how to create *new* self-concepts that reflect our shifting expectations.

Before moving on, please take the time to do the Check Step that follows. You may be amazed at the insights this short exercise can accomplish for you.

CHECK STEP: RESETTING EXPECTATIONS

Step 1: Rewrite the question you wrote for Chapter 6's "Check Step: HAILing Our Wholeness," Step 3.

Step 2: What role will expectations play in your growth? Write a few sentences, draw a picture, or make a collage to capture what comes to mind.

For those who would prefer prompts, spend a moment working through these questions:

1. What expectations do you carry for yourself?
2. Are there expectations that are in flux or have outlived their useful life?
3. Are there expectations that may be holding you back?
4. What is one new expectation you might set for yourself as a part of this growth journey?

Step 3: Rewrite your question from Step 1, taking special care to integrate what you learned about yourself and the expectations you carry. Refer to your answer in Step 2 to support this response.

8

The Incubator:
Reimagining Identity

Who am I? We often ask ourselves such a question in conjunction with an absence: the absence of a once familiar sense of self or when we operate without familiar identity markers, like an occupation or a relationship or a physical capability.

Who am I in the aftermath of a breakup? Who am I without this job that defined a big part of my existence for so long? Who am I if I am no longer physically able to do the kind of things I am used to doing?

Have you ever asked yourself such questions?

The Incubator's next tool helps us create a new relationship with questions like these. Through it, we will create and clarify a new self-concept.

This tool's effectiveness surprised me. Like many, I believed that new forms of self-definition emerged from light-bulb moments or occurred on the heels of something unexpected, like winning the lottery or getting accepted to a selective training program.

What I learned was markedly different. The most consistently reliable way to generate a new self-definition is to interrogate the stories we tell about ourselves and recalibrate the role that our own truth plays in those narratives. As such, this chapter will work on storytelling and teach us how to turn up the volume on our own voices.

A NEW STORY STRUCTURE

As we grow, the stories we tell about ourselves serve as a discovery platform for new self-concepts. Our stories can do the hard work of helping us figure out what to do next. To do so, Incubating requires that we adopt a new story architecture.

Imagine you are tasked with introducing yourself to someone for the first time. Would your first instinct be to rely on a story that features events or circumstances of your life in order of occurrence? If so, you would not be alone. Chronology is by far the most common narrative architecture found in my work.

While common, a chronological story structure can work against us when we grow. It often leaves our listeners off at the moment of a disruptive break, emphasizing uncertainty. It may not surprise you that we reach for the familiarity of this type of structure at times of instability.

While comforting, there is risk in relying on chronological narratives. We are the first and most important audience for our narratives. We internalize these stories and their messages. As such, a reliance on a narrative that emphasizes uncertainty can—in a very insidious fashion—work against us.

The Incubator invites us to change our story's architecture away from chronology and toward a structure that is built around what holds value and meaning to us. For our purposes, we will call this a *value-based* structure.

A NARRATIVE CASE STUDY

Kathleen, a forty-eight-year-old unemployed parent of three children, was surprised by how her self-concept advanced by refocusing her narrative's structure away from chronology and toward value.

I ask Kathleen to introduce herself to me as we sit down. "I had a great run," she starts. "I worked for twenty-six years at a well-known biotech company. I started out as an analyst for our largest product line, then moved into sales, and then I was asked to start two businesses within our largest product line. I was all in. Do not get me wrong. It was *tough*. I loved it. I never minded that vacation was never vacation. I thrived every minute while I worked there." She pauses. "The plan was always to reintegrate the new businesses if we succeeded." She smiles and adds, "What can I say? We did!" The success was bittersweet. "The day the reintegration occurred, my position was eliminated.

"Chapter one of my life's work was great. And I am really proud of chapter one. I want chapter two to look very different. The smart thing to do economically would be to do more of chapter one because that is what I am trained at. But I really do not want chapter two to look anything like chapter one. It is chapter two." She thinks for a moment and offers, "I am having a really hard time figuring out chapter two because I am very proud of what I accomplished. I love my LinkedIn profile. Just freeze it in time." She looks at me sincerely and wonders, "What do I follow it up with?"

I ask Kathleen to talk about how her new status feels. "I am a planner. This is unfamiliar and scary. It is all-consuming. I feel like there are a lot of choices. It makes it harder to define myself."

I give Kathleen a knowing smile and ask her to name a value that she holds dear. "I've always loved creating opportunity for others," says Kathleen. I then ask her to reintroduce herself through the lens of this value.

"I led a new business team that grew from three people to a three-hundred-and-fifty-person organization," she starts. "I love creating opportunities for others. It led me to this leadership role and a track record of success in building and scaling new businesses. I loved every minute. That work completed me. I am excited about the possibility of taking this skill in a new direction, potentially a direction outside of corporate."

She looks at me surprised when she finishes. The comparison is stark. Her second story was about optimism and excitement despite the unknowns she faced.

"This story—the one about creating opportunity for others—surprises me. I am less bothered about the uncertainty of where I am at if I tell it this way." She adds, "This story reminds me that I am bigger than this crisis. It begins a conversation that I was not having before."

Before we move away from Kathleen, I invite us to observe a few takeaways from her story. Kathleen could talk all day long about the chronological details of her career: twenty-six years at one company, the number of businesses started, or how many individual jobs she held over her long tenure. We could listen to that and never learn anything about Kathleen's passion for creating opportunities for others.

By comparison, we learn so much more about who she is when she builds her story upon a value that is important to her. When we step away from chronology and replace it with something we value, we are, by definition, turning up the emphasis on our own truth in our stories. It is impossible for our listener to miss this connection to our passion, our wholeness.

Narratives built around values can feature anything under the sun: a special relationship, a way of being, a curiosity, a faith, or so much more. By relying on such a structure, we engage who we are differently. By relying on this structure, we are turning up the volume on our voices. By referencing voice here, I am not referring to anything audible. I am instead referring to voice as a representation of our truth, our essence. By using a value-based structure, we connect more directly to internal versus external influences. We reduce our susceptibility to uncertainty. And, given that we are our first audience, we open ourselves us up to deeper self-awareness, one that can lead to new, more expansive questions.

In our work thus far, we have revisited again and again this concept of what holds value and meaning to us. For many, these concepts may be on the tip of their tongue. For others, they can be inaccessible or only vaguely familiar. The section that follows serves as a primer on values and meaning for those who find themselves in need of a quick refresher. If you find yourself unsure of what holds value or meaning to you, do not fret. Spend the time to turn your curiosity there. Our work here can help reacquaint you with what you hold true or move you further along in knowing your values.

A PRIMER ON VALUES AND MEANING

Values and meaning play a vital role in our transformation. Through our connection to these, we begin new conversations with ourselves, like Kathleen experienced when she built her story on her love of creating opportunity for others.

Figure 8.1. Common Values.

Values are what we believe to be important. We define them on our own even though we shape them, in part, through cues from our surroundings.

What do you value? What are the most important values you hold now? The word cloud of common values may help you answer these questions (Figure 8.1).[1] Is there anything listed that you call your own?

I invite you to reflect on your values and consider the connection between values and meaning. I link the two in this book because both play a fundamental role in transformation, a process that invites us to come into our voices more fully. Values are a subset of the meaning we hold in our lives. I love the words of John Gardner, founder of Common Cause,[2] in his definition of "meaning":

> Meaning is something you build into your life. You build it out of your own past, out of your affections and loyalties, out of the experience of humankind as it is passed on to you, out of your own talent and understanding, out of the things you believe in and the people you love, out of values for which you are willing to sacrifice something.[3]

Meaning can encompass anything you can imagine and commit yourself to. The one thing to keep in mind is that *all* people, regardless of their circumstances, define meaning in their own way. Therefore, meaning is not for the CEOs of Google or Facebook's Meta or the extraordinary leaders of our time, like Mother Teresa, to determine. Meaning is something everyone—regardless of their socioeconomic circumstances or how they spend their time—must figure out on their own. There is also no prescribed or predetermined "right" meaning. I always hold in my heart the work of *New York Times* investigative journalists Amy Wrzesniewski and Jane Dutton, who remind us that "even for Americans who live frighteningly close to the bone, like janitors, a job is usually more than just a paycheck. It is a source of purpose and meaning."[4]

We all construct and hold our own meaning—everyone, with no exceptions—a concept that guides who we are, how we live our lives, and what growth will entail in our experience.

❖

A REFLECTION: YOUR STORY

This Reflection invites us to reconstitute our stories by using values instead of chronology as the story's architecture. I have found over the last decade that this is one of the surest routes to redefining identity in growth. It is a reliable, fun discovery platform that can be used again and again to explore new self-concepts.

This tool will ask you to reflect on familiar stories you tell about yourself, and it will also direct you to interrogate those stories in a search for important clues. The work here helps you see yourself in a new light and consider how much of yourself you are willing to let others *see* or experience.

Step 1: Tried-and-True

Take a moment to write a chronological introduction for yourself that you might use when meeting someone for the first time. Please try to work with a story that touches upon an area of your identity involved in your transformation.

For example, "Wilma and I met five years ago when we both volunteered at a Habitat for Humanity project outside of Atlanta. We dated for a few years and then she moved away. We got back in touch a year ago when she visited her sister who now lives in my building. We were married three weeks ago."

Step 2: The Limits We Set for Ourselves

Write an internal narrative that you have told yourself but never shared with others. Keep in mind, internal narratives can often be self-limiting.

For example, "My hair is so thin, I am unattractive."

Step 3: Value Narrative

Choose something you value in your life to work with in this exercise. It does not need to be the most important value in your life, nor does it need to be involved directly in your disruption. Rewrite your story from Step 1, only this time, replace chronology with the value you have chosen to work with. Tell the story through the lens of this value.

For example, "Wilma and I are soulmates; we are both so committed to social justice. I knew I was going to marry her the first time I saw her at a Habitat for Humanity volunteer day. We did! Three weeks ago."

Step 4: Observations
Take a moment to reflect on the stories you wrote in response to the above questions.

If you find it useful, answer the following prompts:

- What is the same among your stories?
- What differs across these three stories?
- What does your listener learn about you in each story?
- Through which story does your listener learn the most about you?
- Is there anything missing from all three?
- Where is your truth in each of the stories?

REFLECTION-IN-ACTION

Evelyn, forty-two, a data scientist and parent of three children, was surprised by how powerfully the exercise revealed some ideas about her self-concept.

Her *tried-and-true narrative* was the chronological story she told when interviewing for new work. She was actively looking for a new job after a seven-year absence from the workplace. "I worked for Alphabet right out of school and was recruited by Akamai a few years later," she begins. "I stayed there for five years, then went to Facebook for a short time before I was recruited to join Cloverleaf. It was awesome. A year later, Cloverleaf was acquired by Akamai." Evelyn chuckles a bit, acknowledging how ironic it was to be back working for the same employer she had left years earlier.

"The Cloverleaf acquisition happened when I was out on maternity leave with my youngest. All the Texas employees were either told to relocate or offered packages. I thought I had hit the lottery. I decided to take the package and extend my maternity leave. My plan was to go back to work within six months. That was seven years ago. Early on, it was impossible to make progress finding a new job. My dad got sick and later died from cancer. After that, I applied for jobs but never got much traction. Something always came up in the family. I would never have taken that package had I known it would be this hard to get back in."

Evelyn's *chronological story* was locked tight. She was confident telling it and used it everywhere, from interviewing for new jobs to meeting new people at a yoga studio in town where she volunteered a few hours per month.

Evelyn's *limit narrative* was nothing like the story she told about her work. This story revealed a lifelong battle with her weight. "I never accepted myself. There was always this 'size six' vision of myself that I could never, will never, achieve."

While heartbreaking to hear, Evelyn's awareness of her relationship with her weight proved useful in her next story. After giving some thought to values, she went beyond the workplace linkages she had always relied upon and instead landed on "the importance of the connections" she made related to her own truth.

"A few years ago, I approached the owner of the yoga studio in our town and asked if I could do a session on emotional eating and yoga. It is a spiritual and emotional practice I started when my children were born. This first session turned into more. I have a Facebook page and volunteer at the studio a few hours a week. I love the emotional eating work that I do in my town because it helps me connect with other people; that is my truth: *connecting with others.* I feel as if this work is divinely guided."

Evelyn was surprised by where she landed with the exercise, a deep-seated connection to others. "This looks nothing like I expected. I see that my tried-and-true narrative did little more than emphasize my unplanned seven-year absence from the workplace." She shrugs her shoulders as if now seeing this absence as less of a big deal.

"I am surprised at how strongly my interest in emotional eating came out. I was not seriously considering this type of work before." She stops and then adds, "My voice is strongest there."

Stories anchored by our values help us connect with ourselves in new ways. Reimagining Identity invites us to use our stories as a platform to discover new ideas that can build out an emerging self-concept, one anchored by our growing connection to our truth.

◆

EXTENDED VALUE FROM OUR STORIES

By re-architecting our stories, we gain access to an entirely new way of understanding who we are. We also gain a superpower, a heightened awareness of the stories told by all those around us. Not surprisingly, this heightened awareness helps us ask new questions about ourselves.

By this point in my transformation, my value-based narrative centered on my deepest-held belief: the importance of being seen. In my experience, *being seen* holds two meanings. One is all about my willingness to let others see *who I am*. The other is about my commitment to ensuring that others are seen for *who they are*.

Here is how I tell my story through this lens.

I am thoroughly dedicated to the importance of being seen. So much so that I focus my entire professional self on creating a space for others to draw nearer to who they are and to learn how to live in alignment with that truth—*to be seen*. Today, my work, work that creates this space for others, takes on many forms, from teaching coaches how to support transformational growth in clients, to collaborating with researchers on new ways to think about transformation, and to speaking with audiences about what it means to grow.

This value has been consistent throughout my career, such as in the technology company I founded and in the Fortune 500 company within which I worked. In every employment stop of my career, I was working to make sure someone or some new perspective was seen. Outside of work, I now see a link between this value and the advocacy I've been involved in for the past forty years, first as a feminist and later in support of inclusivity for all marginalized communities.

Working through a value-based narrative helps me access a new way of understanding myself, even now, after working with this material for years. Until I worked with this tool, I never made the connection between my activism and my desire to eradicate the unearned privilege enjoyed by some at the expense of *unseen* others.

This technique also helps me interpret the stories of those around me in a new way, ushering in an awareness I am now ready to address.

My spouse sits next to me at a dinner meeting for parents of boys enrolled in a high school club basketball program. Our son is a new member of this program. Not knowing anyone else at the dinner, we use stories to get to know those around us.

Over the next two hours, my spouse regales the man immediately to his right with stories from our twenty-five-year relationship. In the beginning, I occasionally listen while I chat with those seated closest to me. As the dinner wears on, I turn my attention more carefully in my spouse's direction, alarmed by the snippets I overhear.

He tells the story of visiting Brazil, where I was stationed on an extended work assignment. Despite my work being the reason for this trip, I am *nowhere* in his story.

He describes standing on the deck of a decrepit ferry, watching pink freshwater dolphins dart in and out of the Amazon's muddy brown waters. I do not to hear my name or any reference to my presence. Not once.

Maybe I missed it? I say to myself, deploying the self-effacing behavior I have honed over the years. I listen more intently to make sure I am hearing this correctly.

I can visualize how I was standing right next to him on the deck of that ferry. And yes, it was stunning.

Story after story plays out the same way. I am invisible. Not included in any form.

A pall descends over me. I sit there *silently*. A little dizzy.

This cannot be the first time I am erased in his retelling. I ask myself, *How am I* noticing *his omission of me only now?*

I am stunned by the insights his story offers me.

The waiter arrives to clear the plates. He reaches politely around me to remove my untouched food.

I sit there, awash in a new awareness.

Do I even share a car ride home with this guy, let alone continue sharing my life with him?

◆

A CHECK STEP FOR REIMAGINING IDENTITY

The Incubator's Reimagining Identity relies on stories as a platform for discovery. By re-architecting our stories, we activate more connection with ourselves and turn our curiosity toward wondering how more of our truth might come to light. This story structure broadens our gaze and allows us to ask important new questions about ourselves and that which is occurring all around us.

Re-architecting our stories along value lines offers an entirely different approach to reimagining our identity. It is an accessible, highly reliable method for envisioning a new self-concept. In addition, re-architected stories help us circumvent behaviors that gate off reimagining ourselves until "after . . ." or those that are limited by "past-focused storylines." The ideas that emerge from re-architecting our stories can be simultaneously illuminating and unexpected. The approach contributes to the Incubator's overall goal: to help us to know ourselves in a new way.

In our next chapter, "Reconstituting Connections," we will extend our use of stories and think about how to live in alignment with an emergent self-concept. Please take the time to do the Check Step that follows before moving on.

CHECK STEP: REIMAGINING IDENTITY

Step 1: Restate your final Check Step question from Chapter 7, "Resetting Expectations."

Step 2: What did you learn from the work on your story?

The prompts that follow are offered to help those who would appreciate a little reminder:

- What is your tried-and-true story? How does it differ from your value-based story?
- Did you learn anything new about yourself from your value-based story?
- What role does your voice play in your re-architected story?
- Where might you use your value-based story to the greatest success?
- As a listener, what might I learn about you from your new story? What would remain out of sight?

Step 3: Rewrite your question from Step 1 while taking into consideration what you learned in this chapter. How does your work on your story sharpen the focus of your transformational journey?

9

The Incubator:
Reconstituting Connections

Reconstituting Connections, the final tool in the Incubator's toolkit, works on a truism that can be both surprising and immensely valuable. We get to know more of ourselves through our connections with others. Think about it. We use a newly architected narrative in conversation with others. Through it, they learn more about who we are. They react. They ask questions, and we respond. It is through this give-and-take that we refine our emerging new self-concept and experience what it feels like to live in alignment with our strengthening voices. It is thanks to these exchanges that I hold firm to the notion that we meet ourselves through connections with others.

This chapter explores our connection with others and the role these connections play in our continued advancement. We consider what it means to be "in between" self-concepts and also recognize the connections that can be useful to us at such a time. We will create an In-Between Script, a story you can use with others when you are not sure of where you are or the direction your transformation will lead. This tool anticipates the need for making connections with others throughout a growth process, not gating connections off until sometime in the future when you're at a less uncertain point. This work helps restore our confidence. Like elsewhere in the Incubator, the most beneficial outcome of this tool lies in the questions it helps us ask of ourselves and, in turn, their contribution to our stepping more fully into who we are.

WHAT ARE CONNECTIONS?

Connections are interactions with others that serve as a trial run for our evolving new self-concept. By engaging with others in this fashion, we learn a lot. We find the right words to describe our new status. We experience their reactions, the questions they ask, where they get excited or confused. We also gain a greater intimacy with our own truth.

Think about the connections in Lakshmi's experience. When we met her in Chapter 5, she had left academic medicine and learned, to her very great surprise, that she was considered a funny and insightful leader. This type of discovery is not only something Lakshmi experienced through her connections with others, but it also happened time and again in the stories in my research.

Many of us equate growth with an absence of others. After all, it is common to lose the conduit between ourselves and others as we disengage from once familiar self-concepts. For example, your next-door neighbor may be devastated by his job loss, not only due to his loss of financial security, but also for being deemed ineligible to play on his former employer's softball team. His severed employment eliminated not only his income but also a social structure within which he thrived.

I want to be clear. We are not required to sever relationships with those in our lives because of disruption, like a geographic move. We are instead invited to identify those who can support us. Our decision is far from universal; we may sever ties with some people, we may let other relationships tread water a bit, we may strengthen ties with others, and we may initiate new ones. There is no single "right" answer with respect to relationships. The critical step is identifying those who can support us.

When Justina, forty-nine, unexpectedly lost her job, she became very attuned to the potential for support from the connections she had to those around her. "I have this book club with women that used to be neighbors of mine," she says in recalling a meeting she attended immediately after her loss. "We get together once a month. We've been doing it for fifteen years," she relates proudly. "I'm really close to these women.

"I went to my book club, and I did not say a word about being laid off. I acted as if everything was just normal. I am not in denial, but I am not going to telegraph it. I was not going to tell anybody. I wasn't ready," she continues.

Justina had a keen instinct and was aware of the potential impact others could have on her thinking.

"The few people I have told seem to be very surprised by my termination. They say things like, 'Oh really? You?!'" Their surprise over her job loss was another assault on her already teetering self-esteem.

"I get it. I am learning that 'my people' are not ready for me to be here, let alone be curious. They may never be," she says, a little discouraged.

While Justina veered away from her tried-and-true connections, she found new, more promising ones in a local newcomers' group. She had always been active with the group in spite of living in her town for nearly twenty years. "I am finding people who have been through it. They are the ones."

I ask Justina how it felt to distance herself from those in her book club. She pauses a moment, then says, "I think it is hard on other people. It is very threatening to a lot of people when they hear somebody has veered from a conventional path or that they are searching, really searching, for what is next." She hesitates before continuing. "I am coming to the realization that their reaction is really about them." Justina's observation about others was consistent with many in my research; when it comes to our growth, few of those closest to us are able to think beyond the impact of our decisions on them. They carry a strong need for us to remain the same, a penchant that has them campaign for consistency in our self-definition regardless of the circumstances.

"Growth requires being a little protective of yourself," concludes Justina, "about who you allow in your world and when."

CONNECTING WITH NEW COMMUNITIES

Justina recognized the difference between those who could and could not support her. Many individuals, professionals, and organizations can serve as appreciative communities, those able to support our transformative journey. These communities can be found in a wide variety of places.

Sade, a social worker originally from Fairbanks, Alaska, realized this. With some trepidation, she joined a group I led one evening in the basement of a church in San Francisco's North Beach neighborhood. The day of the event, she sent me a note, "I may not be too talkative but would like to come to listen if you don't mind." Of course, I replied. The next morning, she and I spent time talking one on one.

"I enjoyed last night's conversation. It created a sense of community in the room that cut across all ages and walks of life. I finally get it. I have been in transition for the past twenty years. I made progress, but then something always happened. Personally, I felt that this was so painful and not even understood by close friends and family members. Last night helped me see a way to look for possible answers."

Appreciative communities help us because they stand next to us nonjudgmentally as we turn our curiosity—courageously—toward our sense of self. These communities can be found in lifelong companions, colleagues, and friends, and those who are entirely new to us. The latter often make up the most productive supporters of our growth. New communities know what twelve-step programs, Weight Watchers, and countless other support networks have known for decades. Connecting with others establishes a bridge to ourselves that can bolster self-confidence and positivity at a time these can be lacking.

Sade finishes thoughtfully, "I think people who are going through the same sort of thing as you can kind of relate to a situation whether they know you very well or not. Even if they are different from you, you feel it is kind of the same process, like feeling *I'm not alone in this. I am not the only person that thinks this. It does not make me a bad person,* you know."

Sade, like others in my work, was clear on one thing. "Connections occur anywhere I am not afraid of asking, *What am I doing?* Or, *I thought this is the path that I wanted to be on, but maybe it does not look like what I originally thought.* So, if I take a step back, *it is okay.* These connections know what is going on and, you know, ask if I am okay with the fact that this does not look like the way I thought it would."

There are a few items to be aware of as we think about connecting with appreciative communities: who can serve, our role in the process, and a cautionary note.

WHO CAN SERVE?

The single most important criterion to gauge if someone can serve as a supporter of growth is their ability to ask, "Why not?" Very likely, you will need to look outside your immediate circle for these intrepid souls. Those outside our immediate circle possess a skill that can be easily overlooked: they cannot see our invisible walls.

Close friends and family members—often unknowingly—reinforce restrictive walls around us and carry other biases that make them ineligible to serve as a connection during our growth. They carry a strong need for us to remain the same, a bias that causes them to campaign for consistency in our self-definition regardless of the circumstances.

Our goal for those who accompany us is simple: they need to be inclined to ask, "Why not?" instead of, "Why would you do that?"

Desiree saw the value that can come from looking for support beyond our intimates after participating in one of my focus groups. She offers, "At my age, my mother had three children, a spouse, and a home." In the absence of these milestones, Desiree struggled to keep her perspective.

"I have a good job, but one that I do not like. My dream is to open a dress shop. I love to sew," she confides to those assembled. "I have been thinking about this on and off for years, ever since I earned my degree in textiles," says Desiree.

"Sounds like you do not believe in it," replies Tamara, the woman sitting next to her, matter-of-factly.

Tamara's challenge sent the conversation on an unplanned detour. Desiree and those assembled brainstormed how she might proceed in light of her financial and other obligations. When we turn back to our agenda, Desiree adds, "Thank you!"

"Before today, I never believed I should even try," Desiree continues. "I will start small. I know it is possible." And then she asks, with a slight giggle in her tone, "Would anyone like an appointment?"

Connections help us see beyond the limiting narratives we carry for ourselves, particularly those reinforced by those closest to us.

OUR ROLE

Other people represent only part of the equation for deriving value from connections. The other part of the equation is *us*. To Reconstitute Connections, we need to not only activate our truth but also be willing to let others experience it. The term often used to describe these steps is *agency*, or a willingness to act on our own behalf.

I find it very useful to think about "our role" in connections as a willingness to adopt certain behaviors that reflect our emerging truth. This is separate and apart from knowing our truth. I think of Pascal, whom we met in Chapter 7, who shared with us the story of his coming out. He knew for a long time his truth, that of being a gay man, yet for him, it was an additional series of steps to tell others and still more steps to fully live in alignment with that truth.

As we grow, we advance along these two dimensions: we know more of our truth, and we increase our willingness to act in alignment with that truth. Each in our own circumstances has to decide how to behave along both of these dimensions.

Think about the advances Desiree made as she connected with others. She clarified more about her self-concept as she explored her interest in textiles in a new way. This step helped her believe, for the first time, that it was possible to live with her passion within the constraints imposed by her personal situation. She took steps to think through what it might mean to bring her truth to life. She began to live in alignment with this belief as she lightheartedly asked who wanted an appointment, a small but meaningful step.

Coming to know our truth and acting in alignment with it is an exciting and expansive process, one that can be supported by many others. As we learn to trust ourselves and others via connections, their contributions can serve as an accelerator in our progress.

A CAUTIONARY NOTE

During times of uncertainty, we run the risk of relying too much on the opinions of others. In fact, I am surprised by how often I hear stories of folks for whom connections prove limiting. It mostly occurs when we look to others to fill in the blanks left open as we re-examine and update our self-definition.

My heart sinks when an excited individual who is pursuing growth tells me, "I met with such and such poo-bah. He thinks I should do [X]. I am going to do it. I am so excited."

Let us face it, it is easy to cede our ground to others when someone purports to "know" what we should do. Their certainty can feel like a safe haven in a turbulent storm of change and uncertainty.

Always keep in mind that no one can know what is in your heart unless you do the work to know yourself and choose to tell them. However difficult it is to conjure what you love, believe in, or care about, you are the only one who can start that conversation.

THE VALUE OF OTHERS

When they work—which they frequently do—connections add irreplaceable value to our journey. Serena, fifty-one, a twice-divorced woman who had one grown son, found herself grateful for the unexpected contribution of others. She lost her job on the heels of a merger between her employer and another large company. "I always imagined I had many more years of employment to get my financial house in order," says Serena, still surprised by this turn of events months later. "The layoff was unexpected. It's been stressful, particularly financially."

Serena thrived for years on corporate America's outsized demands. "Nearly sixty hours a week," she recalls of her work schedule, "once I factor in the hour-long commute each way.

"I am surprised by how quickly the importance of that world fell away once I was outside of it. I was always running to the next thing: the quarterly revenue targets, the stretch performance goals, the invite-only meetings, the client events. I was always *on*.

"I am a big believer in self-care. I took time for some of that after it happened," she says of a two-month cleanse she took to recuperate from the pace of her life pre-termination.

"I kept asking myself, *What's next?* There was no going back." Unsure about what the future could offer, she turned to volunteerism to connect with others while she figured it out.

"I volunteered with a group of pet owners in town who maintain a dog park," she says, referencing her love of animals. "I went to meetings and helped get some important support from town officials," she offers in a tone as if saying, *Nothing special.*

"In hindsight, my self-esteem got a much-needed boost from my involvement with the park. I am so grateful to the people I met there. My former colleagues did not get it." She pauses and adds sincerely, "They did not understand why I was still looking for my 'next thing.' Being accepted when I felt outside my former circle was crucial," says Serena. "That boost helped me believe I could do something very different for work."

The confidence boost did not immediately extinguish Serena's financial worry. "It has taken a lot longer than I originally anticipated to find a new job. My connections with other people—people new to me—are what got me through.

"I accepted a role with an animal rights organization last week," offers Serena, smiling. "This whole cycle has taught me something. We come back to ourselves, only better."

A NEW BRIDGE

Connections with others pay dividends beyond an immediate interaction if we allow our truth to play a central role. By leading with our truth, these connections help us understand ourselves in new ways. Mei, a fifty-nine-year-old single woman, was emboldened by this shift and the impact it had on her thinking and life.

Mei's family immigrated to the United States in the early 1970s when she and her sister were nine. "Our community is very family-centric. We take care of one another. I have a deep devotion to my sister and to my parents' memory.

"My sister, Aiko, and I are very close; neither of us is married. Aiko never married, and my husband died more than a decade ago," says Mei. She was happy to care for her sister but realized that *how* she cared for Aiko needed to change.

Aiko recently had a heart attack and moved in with Mei after being discharged from a convalescent care unit at a local hospital. Aiko's needs had always taken precedence in their relationship, a pattern Mei attributed to their doting, careful parents and Aiko's health challenges as a young child.

Mei saw parallels between her role in her sister's care and a stressful period in her life years earlier. A decade before Aiko's illness, Mei lost her job as an administrator for a large defense contractor. She loved her work and was proud to contribute to such a large corporation. When the unexpected layoff occurred, Mei's world was thrown out of balance. "I could not believe when it happened to me. Maybe I was even a little ashamed. I had been with the company for a long time," recalls Mei, sadly.

She pauses and observes, "After I lost my job, my voice changed." She surprises me with what comes next. "I let others see my creativity and compassion. My voice quieted, too. Not that I did not speak. I became more attuned to the needs of those around me. That never felt possible in my job. All of a sudden, I did not need to be in charge. It allowed more of me to show up."

Mei experienced even more changes in her voice tied to her changing relationship with Aiko and Aiko's growing care needs. Mei knew that these more recent changes were more substantive than even those she experienced when she lost her job. She says, "I am more courageous. I am more aware of what is important to me, and I am willing to let those needs come into my relationships in small ways." Mei credited the values and expectations work in Resetting Expectations for kick-starting this shift.

"After the first six months of my sister's care, I bravely talked to Aiko about what I needed in the relationship, too," says Mei. "It was the first time I brought what was important to me into the discussion. I talked about my need to make time for my gardening and for volunteering at a local community food bank. I started volunteering there after I lost my job many years ago. My relationships to the people there are incredibly important to me." The sisters worked out a schedule to support Mei. "It was not much, but I got some important respite," offers Mei softly.

"Creating new space for me, for more of me, in the relationship with Aiko was like resetting a table that had been set a certain way for fifty years," says Mei. "This might sound small, but it changed everything."

NAVIGATING "IN BETWEEN"

While others have the potential to contribute enormously to our transformation, it is not always obvious what to say to them. After all, what do we say to others when we are not even sure of the answers ourselves?

Katrinka and her husband of thirty years divorced two years after her youngest started college. She withdrew from others as she found

---

'How To' Transform Ourselves

- We **re-examine** beliefs, values, and expectations that constitute all or part of who we are.

- We **reframe** emotions that can mobilize to keep us in place.

- We **revitalize and/or create** new beliefs, values, and expectations for ourselves.

- We **disengage** from values, beliefs, and expectations that no longer serve us.

- We **integrate** these new and refined expectations, values, and beliefs into a new self-concept.

- We **act** in accordance with this new self-concept.

Figure 9.1. "How To" Transform Ourselves.

herself *in between*, a painful and embarrassing state for which she had no words.

"What am I going to say?" she offers rhetorically as she describes the potential of running into people she knew around town. After a moment's pause, she adds, "You know, if they don't have a half-hour, I don't know how I would tell them where I am at." I understood her frustration, shared by many who navigate relationships during disruption.

She continues, "Those I have told ask me, 'What do *you* want?'" emphasizing her role in the decision. "I do not even know how to answer that question for myself. What am I supposed to say to someone else?"

My hope is that we can create a script that will allow us to connect with others even when it feels, as Katrinka was describing, as if it is near impossible to speak with others about where we are at. I use the term "in between" to represent these times that can occur at any time throughout our transformational growth process, beginning with steps we take to re-examine our sense of self and continuing to the end of the cycle when we act in accordance with a newly minted self-definition (Figure 9.1). Anywhere along this continuum, we can experience quite a conundrum: we are not sure what to say about where we are, and yet, we need others to help us clarify our truth.

To support us in this liminal space, we will create an "In-Between Script" to get us beyond the negativity often ascribed to our uncertain status. The script can be used by anyone who is progressing along a growth path: when "in between jobs," "in between relationships," or "in between" anything else.

A REFLECTION: CREATING YOUR IN-BETWEEN SCRIPT

What do you say to someone when you are in the throes of incubating? The answer lies in developing a script that honors the work you are doing and engages others in your self-exploratory process.

Many confuse an In-Between Script with a "personal elevator pitch," or a story with a few sentences that summarizes who you are professionally and the value you or your company will deliver. Such elevator pitches emerged from the iconic Silicon Valley tech founders who prepared them in hopes of landing in an elevator with potential investors. Our In-Between Script creates a story structure that draws your listener into a conversation, allowing you to gain valuable feedback about your journey.

Step 1: Write a word or phrase that summarizes the last question you created in support of your growth journey. Refer to the Check Steps in Chapters 6, 7, and 8.

For example, Katrinka's might be, "I am thinking about who I am beyond this marriage."

Step 2: Now use the Mad Libs structure that follows to create an In-Between Script by *circling* the appropriate word from the word banks and *filling* in the blanks.

I am [choose one: exploring, investigating, researching, wondering about, preparing for, working on, testing, hoping to, building a plan for, considering, learning about, taking steps toward, starting to frame out, or curious about] _____ [insert answer from Step 1]. It is part of a larger effort to [choose one: address, move beyond, explore, help, figure out, understand, reset after, take a breath after, or envision] _____ [fill in a headline that summarizes your disruption. Refer to Chapter 1, Step 1].

Step 3: What are the conditions under which you would be successful using this script?

For those who might find it useful, answer these prompts:

- Where or when would it be possible to use this script?
- Who is with you? Is anyone absent?
- How does it feel to use this script?
- What else needs to happen in order for you to comfortably use this script?

- What do others learn about you from your script?
- What about you might remain hidden from your listener?
- What might you do to increase the likelihood of success in using the script?

REFLECTION-IN-ACTION

Victor reported some real trepidation about using his In-Between Script. He lived in Dallas in a converted warehouse not far from the American Airlines Center where his beloved Dallas Mavericks played.

Victor, an accountant, resigned from a corporate position to become an entrepreneur eighteen months before we spoke. His move was a big decision, one that he hoped would begin to pay off soon.

The excitement of the early days had waned. "I am getting concerned," he starts. "Things are taking a lot longer than I ever imagined." Victor responds to this situation by working more, doubling down on his commitment to bringing his dream to life. "Over the past six months, I withdrew more and more into my work. My whole world is the company, two part-time developers, and me.

"I keep wondering, *Did I make a huge mistake leaving my job?*" says Victor rhetorically.

At the urging of his girlfriend, Thalia, Victor begrudgingly attended a dinner party. "I decided to go for it," he says, describing his first time using his In-Between Script. "I abandoned my standard story, 'I am working on a start-up,' and instead used the script."

"'I am *working on* a new app for making big-ticket purchases at large companies. It is part of my interest in *exploring* how companies can use technology in decision-making.' I lived this day-in and day-out when I was working. No company I ever worked for got this right. It is a huge opportunity. I resigned and started over a year ago to pursue this full time."

To his great surprise, Victor's story took center stage and prompted dinner conversation for the remainder of the evening. All assembled had something to add. He left the dinner energized for the first time in longer than he could remember.

Connections, like the ones Victor made at a chance dinner party, are not an end to our process. They provide oxygen and light as we gain the confidence to engage more of who we are in our interactions with others. In these situations, we are reminded that growth rests on our willingness to lead with who we are.

◆

THE ENDURING VALUE OF CONNECTIONS

Incubating, as Mei and Victor learned, invites us to bring more of who we are into interactions with others, a courageous step that benefits our growth in many ways. Through our interactions with others, we not only learn about ourselves but also establish important new connections with others.

I learned this, too, thanks to a deepening connection to my truth and my willingness to live in alignment with my growing voice in all corners of my life.

Three years after my first book was published, I was invited to join the board of a global women's organization of which I am a member. "YES!" was my answer, with only one caveat. I wanted to be involved in programming. I had by then amassed quite an experience base in how to engage large groups in interactive activities that facilitate their connection to themselves and one another. What is it that they say, *Be careful what you ask for?* I was named co-chair of programming for the organization.

Every year, the group hosts an event on March 8 in honor of International Women's Day. On that day, like many similar organizations, this group typically hosts panel discussions during which influential people are invited to talk with the members. "Who can we get to speak?" asked our colleagues of my co-chair and me months before the date. You can imagine that finding great speakers for that day is like attempting to hire a gifted actor for a gig on the afternoon of the Oscars.

I had an idea for a new type of event thanks to trusting my inner voice. I ran it by my co-chair. What if we held an event that featured the voices of our members? The organization had more than eight thousand members, people who were extraordinarily gifted and making an impact on our world in their own unique ways. Instead of doing a one-panel event on March 8, we could feature a voice of one of our members every day over the course of the month. "31 Voices" emerged as a daily celebration of the diversity within our membership and as an entrée for members to connect with one another.

We put together a talented working group to bring the idea to life. What emerged from that collaboration was a truly unique event. Members interested in serving as one of the 31 Voices filled out an application that asked them to describe themselves, the greatest influences in their lives, and the wisdom they would like to share with others.

From the submitted applications, we chose thirty-one dynamic women who would be featured daily on social media, in newsletters, and on our website. Most importantly, all members, both featured and participants, would be encouraged to connect with one another and needed only to take a simple step—to click—to initiate such a connection.

The idea was like the progressive dinner parties common in the 1990s when neighborhoods would get together and each apartment or house would host a different part of the meal. The rolling nature of the program overcame geographic limitations and did not rely on a single celebrity speaker or preferred time zones. "31 Voices" was quickly embraced by our membership.

The Incubator informed nearly every aspect of how I showed up to contribute to this program, from the application requirements we set for speakers, to the opportunity created for members to connect with one another. The program elevated everyone's voice, far more than thirty-one single voices. It created a platform upon which members could experience another's truth and use that visibility to initiate an authentic connection.

After its conclusion, members wrote to thank the organization and share all manner of excitement about what they learned. One very special note came from a woman whose spouse was undergoing cancer treatment over the thirty-one days. It said, "You belong to the angels in my life."

The Incubator allowed me to operate at that very special level: a place of energy and light accessible when we operate in alignment with our voices. Anyone who commits the time to use the Incubator's tools can benefit in a similar fashion.

Most importantly, I was surprised at how easy it felt to contribute to activities, like "31 Voices," once I completed the Incubator's steps. This relative ease underscores a simple truth: when we are aligned with our voices, we shine without even trying.

◆

CHECK STEP: RECONSTITUTING CONNECTIONS

I hope after reading this chapter you have a new understanding of what I mean when I say, "We meet ourselves through our connection with others." If we are willing to bring more and more of our truth to our interactions with others, we gain self-confidence and establish a deeper connection to who we are.

This chapter's embrace of connections and their role in our journey invites us to engage who we are—at whatever point we are in our evolution. By connecting with others in our growth process, we learn how to trust our newly envisioned selves.

Step 1: Rewrite your final question from the Chapter 8 Check Step or the most recent Check Step you completed.

Step 2: Write a sentence or two about what you learned about your journey through this chapter's discussion of connections.

If you would prefer working with prompts, try answering these questions:

- What is your In-Between Script about?
- What does a listener learn about you through your In-Between Script?
- How willing are you to share your voice with others?
- Who might be able to serve as a connection for you?
- Where might you find that person(s)?
- Where and with whom has your truth been most clear? Most absent?

Step 3: Rewrite the question that guides your transformative journey by integrating your responses to Steps 1 and 2.

10

Your Enriching Journey

"When does it end?" I am on the receiving end of this question all the time in my work. I get it. Growth is invigorating, enlivening, hopeful, and optimistic. It can also be demanding, confusing, isolating, and emotionally charged. Who would not want to get through it as quickly as possible?

I often hesitate in answering the question, fearful over how it might land. Once we begin a cycle of transformative growth, our progression never ends.

What do you mean it never ends? Let's agree. This answer can feel overwhelming.

Here is the good news in all of this. Once we initiate a growth cycle, the connectedness it establishes between us and our truth remains a constant.

Our gaze is forever changed by growth. There may be times when the cycle is less active, but its imprint is unwavering. Those who have walked this way in advance of us credit the journey with delivering joy, peace, exhilaration, and enduring strength to their lives.

In this chapter, we will explore the many gifts available to those willing to embark on such a growth journey. We will review the key takeaways from our work together, and we will end with a special story about the gifts available to all who open themselves up to leading with who they are.

AN INVALUABLE GIFT

Disruption occurs continuously throughout our lives. Those disruptions that influence our sense of self and/or impact our functioning offer us something extraordinary: an opportunity to make a choice that can positively influence the trajectory of our lives. I know this is a strong claim. I make it carefully as I have witnessed time and again the many gifts that accrue to those who journey this way. The gifts express themselves in tangible ways, like new jobs or new apartments, but more importantly in intangible ways, like greater self-knowledge, improved self-confidence, increased positivity, an updated definition of success, and a higher comfort level with uncertainty.

Lakshmi, whom we met in Chapter 5 when she left academic medicine, joined me to talk about the gifts she realized thanks to her courageous steps along a transformational path. We met at a little coffee shop near her home on Chicago's Near North Side.

"I think our inner voice is both our most profound and enduring critical success factor," she says, and then adds philosophically, "Once we are aware of our inner voice, we are really perpetually in states of growth.

"I don't mean that we are always actively disengaging from something because so often we can't," continues Lakshmi. "We can't afford to disengage economically, psychologically, spiritually, whatever. I think transformation activates a part of our nature, and I actually think it is part of our brain chemistry, which is continually bridging us from one state to something *more*. Once it started for me, there was a whole new level of consciousness," Lakshmi adds smiling. "I would never have gotten here without the many steps that led me away from pain and toward possibility."

Lakshmi's beliefs about growth confirmed what I observed through the many conversations I have been fortunate enough to have had through my research. Once we initiate a cycle of transformative growth, we open ourselves up to an ever-broadening path of moving closer and closer to our fullness. This increased proximity to our voices bestows upon us an unbridled energy that plays out in every corner of our lives. We never step away from who we are once we activate our voices. We can learn to turn up the volume, but we are never muted.

"We still have to adapt to our culture, the people around us," offers Lakshmi, "and their demands." She reflects a moment and adds, "I am now so aware of my new assumptions. I bring them to all situations. My growth is a ritual, in a way. Coming into my truth and allowing it to be present changes everything."

Lakshmi's words remind me of a simple truth. Through transformational growth, we establish an unbreakable bond between ourselves and our own voices. Through it, we greet ourselves and the world differently.

Lakshmi smiles and hands me a little gift as our conversation draws to a close. It looks as if it is a large piece of paper she has folded into an impossibly small square, about the size of a 3×3 Post-It note. I feel so touched by this gesture. I'm reminded of our first interview years earlier, when I had asked her to name a gift she would give to someone starting out on their journey.

I unfold Lakshmi's treat carefully. A map of the world emerges. "Thank you," she says to me in a near whisper as I take in the beauty of this ornately colored map.

Lakshmi had her map. She was gifting this one to me for others.

YOUR POSSIBILITY

Disruptions occur all around us. Some disruptions impact our ability to function and/or influence our thinking about our sense of self. Those that do represent an unlikely invitation, one that invites us to connect with ourselves and the world in new ways. These disruptions serve as a gateway to unforeseen possibilities in our lives.

I will never forget how it felt to experience such a disruption without the understanding of what was happening. It was frightening and chaotic in ways I had never experienced before. Even more striking, I never heard the word "growth" from *any* of the many colleagues, advisors, peers, and neighbors to whom I had reached out to help me get my bearings at that time. Not one.

In hindsight, I am not surprised. Societal norms reward us for looking through, tamping down, or running at full speed in the other direction at such times. In fact, individuals who honor such disruptions are often ridiculed, shunned, or led to believe that they carry some type of irreparable flaw. My research contradicts these societal norms and underscores the fact that these gateway disruptions offer unprecedented opportunities to access the untapped capacity that lives within each of us.

How will we respond to such disruptions? If we pursue *change*, we leave intact our assumptions about who we are, a choice that favors stability in our self-concept. If we pursue *transition*, we re-examine the assumptions upon which our sense of self relies, a choice that welcomes instability in our self-concept for a time. This choice, the choice of transition, enables transformational growth. While demanding, this type of growth is enlivening and draws forward the unique, resplendent qualities that constitute the fullness of who we are.

Transformational growth involves updating the inputs upon which we rely to set our expectations for and definition of who we are. At the outset of such a process, our sense of self is typically built upon external influences and mirrors the beliefs of others, including—but not limited to—the beliefs held by our families, the schools we attend, the occupations we choose, and those we love. As we update our self-concept, we replace those external influences with self-defined beliefs, those that more accurately reflect that which holds value and meaning to us. We discover more about our unique inner voice and disengage from the expectations of others we uncritically adopted along the way. If we continue to grow beyond this point, we can add additional inputs upon which our sense of self can rely; those we add put us on a transcendent path and reflect an embrace of the interconnectedness of all humanity.

Our emotions play a starring role in our experience of disruption and throughout our growth journey. Emotions mobilize to keep us safe as we disengage from familiar expressions of who we are. When we move away from familiar identity markers, like a relationship or a hometown, our emotions read this break from the familiar as *unsafe*. I always imagine this response as our emotions acting like a caring friend who asks, "Are you sure?" before we disengage from familiar expressions of ourselves in favor of something new and unknown. The great news, of course, is that we need not be stopped by these emotions. We can learn to reframe them such that we can be successful in light of their presence.

The Incubator is our transformational growth toolkit that empowers us to turn innovation toward our sense of self. Through it, we reframe emotions, update the expectations we carry for ourselves, create a new self-concept, and connect with others—and ourselves—via new expressions of who we are. The toolkit is built upon key concepts that can serve us well throughout our growth journey: a reliance on awareness techniques, an embrace of informed experimentation, and an unshakable belief in the value of the questions we ask ourselves.

Through transformative growth, we learn to lead with who we are.

COMING INTO OUR TRUTH

Our truth is affirmed in ways big and small throughout our transformational journey. These opportunities—however they arrive—help us spread our wings further and access the energy and spirit that accrue to those who courageously walk along this path. I was reminded of this value during a memorable visit with a dear friend.

I drove down to New York to visit Claire, who was then fifty-three, on Valentine's Day. She was sequestered at her aunt's house while on the waiting list for a lung transplant.

"Waiting."

What an awful word.

Claire is single and someone I have known for thirty years. I have always been amazed at her connection with her family; she is the emotional glue for her three brothers and their families along with countless cousins, nieces, and nephews.

Claire's illness, a by-product of an earlier victory over breast cancer, turned the tables upside down on her and her extended family. Waiting was crushing everyone. Would she be there to glam it up with her niece in prom pictures that spring? Would she play kickball, her all-time favorite sport, at the family's summer picnic?

When I arrive, I am struck by Claire's appearance. Her usual all-put-together self, the bold one that donned mini-dresses and fringe-laced halter tops while we were in graduate school, is absent. Missing too is her ready smile. In its place sits a woman with severely darkened eye sockets and a grayness to her pallor that is unsettling. She asks me to sit close. I pull up a folding chair and hold her hand in mine.

Claire is sleepy, exhaustion being a common symptom of severe breathing problems. As she dozes in and out, I recall a long-ago time when she landed in what looked to be a safe place after beating breast cancer. She told me then, "I operated for a while with a unilateral focus." That focus was her treatment. "It was terrifying and uncertain," she had said, "but strangely, it liberated me from other stuff."

Once through that treatment, everyone, except her, was celebrating her victory. "Directionless" was how she described it to me. Claire felt as if she was sitting on the sidelines with a mix of enthusiasm for having beaten cancer and of confusion over a vexing dilemma that, at the time, felt cruel. "*Who am I?*" she kept repeating during that time way back when.

I run to Jamba Juice for our lunch when it looks as if her dozing has given way to a real nap. She is alert when I return.

"How did you do it?" she asks me in a tone that I know cannot mean the speediness with which I returned with our smoothies. "What?" I ask casually, although I can sense where she is heading.

"I cannot function on the surface this way," she says flatly. "My brothers call, but all they talk about is my care: 'Did I take my medicine?' 'Did I speak with Dr. Richie?' 'What did she say?' There is never time for more." I know the brothers. They are overwhelmed, hardly functioning in the wake of Claire's diagnosis.

Claire is suddenly aware of the expectations that feel out of whack, those she carries for herself and the ones carried by those around her. Her new awareness helps her ask different questions about her proximity to her own truth and her relationships with others.

Claire's question is incredibly special to me. With it, she acknowledges that I operated in a different place for a long time, one she had never been aware of even though she walked right next to me. How could she—and I—miss what was happening to me in plain sight? Her use of the past tense honors my journey. She *sees* me now in a different, fuller, more expansive light, an outcome of dancing with disruption.

I sit closer and listen carefully. She rants about how her brothers' behavior falls short. "What about *me?*" she says as her voice rattles. She is using a new lens through which to see herself and her connection to others.

"Why is this time so different?" Claire asks as she squeezes my hand more tightly and looks directly into my eyes. "*Why now? Why this one?*"

I know she is not looking for an answer. "I got through cancer, the death of both of my parents." She ticks off a few more disruptive moments we had shared over the past decades. "Even though I said the words, I am not sure I ever really questioned *who I am.* I was always able to hang on to some semblance of my identity.

"This time . . ." Her voice trails off. She is quiet again. Minutes later, she is asleep.

Yes, this time is different. Not for the profile of her diagnosis or the recovery we all await; this time is different because she is aware of something new, she is asking herself different questions, and most importantly, she has the tools to access the possibility she can sense in her heart.

Claire sleeps for most of the remainder of the afternoon. We do not get to say much more before I leave.

A few days later, I received a handwritten note from her.

"Your work—and your own journey—inspire me to live more bravely and to look to the future with hope and positivity. It has boosted my confidence. I am so much better now despite the reality of my diagnosis. That may be hard to understand, even for me, it is."

MY GIFT FOR YOU

I wish for you an unfettered connection to who you are and a willingness to trust your truth in all the circumstances of your life. The world urgently needs your voice—regardless of its expression or stage of completion.

Remember to welcome shifts in your self-concept, as they can be precursors to positive improvements in your life. At those moments, make informed choices, ones that honor your firm understanding of disruption and transformative growth.

If you embrace transition as opposed to change, your choice will nourish you and deepen your connection to yourself and others. Greet what you learn on this journey with an open heart. Your willingness to do so will dramatically alter your experience, the experience of those with whom you come in contact, and the well-being of our world at large.

Please know that if you trust our work together and choose to live in alignment with who you are, you move along a path of light even on a cloudy day.

No matter where you are on your journey—at its outset or well into its progression—I hope you hold onto the words that Claire chose in the closing of her note to me.

"Keep in mind, *you* are loved."

Notes

CHAPTER 1

1. The Rosetta Stone, discovered in 1799, allowed archeologists to crack the code of the Egyptian hieroglyphics. https://www.history.com/news/what-is-the-rosetta-stone.

CHAPTER 2

1. Self-sameness is championed as a developmental concept by researchers from the Netherlands, including Anna Lichtwarck-Aschoff and Paul van Geert, "Time and Identity: A Framework for Research and Theory Formation," *Developmental Review* 28, no. 3 (2008): 370–400.

2. The concept of a protective response is derived from the work of psychiatrist Roger Gould. He is a leading authority on adult development. Roger Gould. 1978. *Transformations: Growth and Change in Adult Life*. New York: Simon & Schuster.

3. Jennifer Ouellette. 2014. *Me, Myself, and Why: Searching for the Science of Self*. Penguin Books. Page 3.

4. Derived from Shari Lewchanin and Louise Zubrod, "Choices in Life: A Clinical Tool for Facilitating Midlife Review," *Journal of Adult Development* 8, no. 3 (2001).

CHAPTER 3

1. The terms "beliefs," "values," and "expectations" are used extensively throughout Professor Marcia Baxter Magolda's 2009 book *Authoring Your Life*. Her groundbreaking longitudinal research of college students and how they progress through developmental milestones began in 1986 and continued for decades. She is a Distinguished Professor Emerita at Miami University of Ohio and has written extensively on developmental progression through adulthood. She joins other distinguished scholars, including Robert Kegan and Lisa Laskow Lahey, who similarly view transformative growth as a function of how individuals set their definition of and expectations for the self. Their prolific work is best summarized in the 2009 book *Immunity to Change*.

2. Carol Gilligan's 1982 book, *In a Different Voice*, positions transformational growth as an act of summoning into awareness an individual's previously disassociated voice.

3. This reference is taken from Sue Monk Kidd's compelling story of transformational growth chronicled in *The Dance of the Dissident Daughter: A Woman's Journey from Christian Tradition to the Sacred Feminine* (2016, HarperOne). The reference is taken from pages 9 and 55.

4. Scott Barry Kaufman. 2020. *Transcend: The New Science of Self-Actualization*. TarcherPerigee. Page 233. Derived from Professor Kaufman's careful review and modern interpretation of Maslow's work.

CHAPTER 4

1. Antonio Damasio. 1999. *The Feeling of What Happens: Body and Emotion in the Making of Consciousness*. Harcourt Brace & Co. Pages 50–51.

2. Ibid. Page 8.

3. Derived from the Hoffman Institute Foundation. Tara Parker-Pope. "First, Try to Identify and Name That Emotion." *New York Times*, May 25, 2021.

4. Joanne Cacciatore. 2017. *Bearing the Unbearable: Love, Loss, and the Heartbreaking Path of Grief*. Wisdom Publications. Pages 54–58.

CHAPTER 5

1. Y Combinator, https://www.ycombinator.com/.

CHAPTER 6

1. Cacciatore, Joanne. 2017. *Bearing the Unbearable: Love, Loss, and the Heartbreaking Path of Grief.* Wisdom Publications. Page 131.

2. Check steps serve as a valuable management technique. In the technology industry, new products get created over many months. To keep large teams working effectively over these extended time periods, check steps are performed at the end of each day to achieve two goals: to integrate all of the work completed by individuals that day, and to highlight any potential conflicts across the work of many individual contributors. This practice serves as a critical success determinant; a breakthrough made by one developer on any given day can be shared with others by the start of the next business day. For our work, similar breakthroughs are possible.

CHAPTER 7

1. *The Sound of Music* LP is a recording format of the musical by the same name. LP stands for long play. These twelve-inch records were played at 33 1/3 rpm. The album features the musical score from the 1965 film starring Julie Andrews and Christopher Plummer. https://www.sound-of-music.com/sound-of-music/the-movie/.

CHAPTER 8

1. Derived from "Merging Two Worlds: A Two-Tier Model for Transitioning Youth." 2003. *Empower Your Life*, Chapter 1, Lesson 2, Empower Your Future: A career readiness curriculum. Both curricula are developed and made available through GCFGlobal.org.

2. https://www.commoncause.org/.

3. Elizabeth White. 2019. 55, *Underemployed, and Faking Normal: Your Guide to a Better Life.* Simon & Schuster. Page 83.

4. Charles Duhigg. "The Future of Work: Wealthy, Successful, and Miserable." *New York Times*, February 24, 2019.

Bibliography

Allen, Catherine, Nancy Bearg, Rita Foley, and Jaye Smith. 2011. *Reboot Your Life*. New York: Beaufort Books.

Ammerman, Colleen, and Boris Groysberg. 2021. *Glass Half Broken: Shattering the Barriers That Still Hold Women Back at Work*. Boston, MA: Harvard Business Review Press.

Bardwick, Judith. 1979. *In Transition: How Feminism, Sexual Liberation, and the Search for Self-Fulfillment Have Altered Our Lives*. New York: Holt, Rinehart and Winston.

Baxter Magolda, Marcia. 2009. *Authoring Your Life: Developing Your Internal Voice to Navigate Life's Challenges*. Sterling, VA: Stylus Publishing.

Baxter Magolda, Marcia B. 2001. *Making Their Own Way: Narratives for Transforming Higher Education to Promote Self-Authorship*. Sterling, VA: Stylus Publishing.

Belenky, Mary Field, Blythe McVicker Clinchy, Nancy Rule Goldberger, and Jill Mattuck Tarule. 1997. *Women's Way of Knowing: The Development of Self, Voice, and Mind*. New York: Basic Books.

Ben-Shahar, Tal. 2007. *Happier: Learn the Secrets to Daily Joy and Lasting Fulfillment*. New York: McGraw Hill.

Blake, Jenny. 2016. *Pivot: The Only Move That Matters Is Your Next Move*. New York: Portfolio/Penguin.

Brach, Tara. 2019. *Radical Compassion: Learning to Love Yourself and Your World with the Practice of RAIN*. New York: Viking.

Brach, Tara. 2012. *True Refuge: Finding Peace and Freedom in Your Own Awakened Heart*. New York: Random House.

Brewer, Judson. 2021. *Unwinding Anxiety: New Science Shows How to Break the Cycles of Worry and Fear to Heal Your Mind*. New York: Penguin Random House.

Bridges, William. 2004. *Transitions: Making Sense of Life's Changes, 25th Anniversary Edition*. Boston, MA: Da Capo Lifelong.

Bridges, William, and Susan Bridges. 2016. *Managing Transitions: Making the Most of Change*. Boston, MA: Da Capo Lifelong.

Brody, Jane E. "Making Meaning Out of Grief: Getting On with Life after a Loved One's Death Is a Complex Multi-Step Process." *New York Times*, November 5, 2019.

Brooks, Arthur. "Sit with Negative Emotions, Don't Push Them Away." *The Atlantic*, June 18, 2020.

Brown, Brené. 2007. *I Thought It Was Just Me (But It Isn't): Making the Journey from "What Will People Think?" to "I Am Enough."* New York: Avery.

Brown, Lyn Mikel, and Carol Gilligan. 1993. *Meeting at the Crossroads: Women's Psychology and Girls' Development*. New York: Ballantine Books.

Buckingham, Marcus, and Donald Clifton. 2001. *Now, Discover Your Strengths*. New York: The Free Press.

Burnett, Bill, and Dave Evans. 2018. *The Designing Your Life Workbook: A Framework for Building a Life You Can Thrive In*. New York: Clarkson Potter Publishers.

Burnham, Sophy. 2011. *The Art of Intuition: Cultivating Your Inner Wisdom*. New York: Jeremy P. Tarcher/Penguin.

Burns, David D. 1999. *The Feeling Good Handbook*. New York: Plume Penguin Random House.

Burton, Mary Lindley, and Richard Wedemeyer. 1991. *In Transition: From the Harvard Business School Club of New York's Career Management Seminar*. New York: Harper Business.

Cacciatore, Joanne. 2017. *Bearing the Unbearable: Love, Loss, and the Heartbreaking Path of Grief*. Somerville, MA: Wisdom Publications.

Cameron, Julia. 2016. *The Artist's Way: A Spiritual Path to Higher Creativity, 25th Anniversary Edition*. New York: TarcherPerigee Books.

Cameron, Julia. 1992. *The Artist's Way Workbook*. New York: Jeremy P. Tarcher/Penguin.

Chocano, Carina. "Conventional Wisdom: Why Do We Universalize the 'Experience' of Half the World—and Obscure, Deny and Control That of the Other?" *New York Times Magazine*, October 28, 2018.

Chodron, Pema. 2016. *When Things Fall Apart: Heart Advice for Difficult Times*. Berkeley, CA: Shambala.

Choquette, Sonia. 1997. *Your Heart's Desire: Instructions for Creating the Life You Really Want*. New York: Potter Style.

Clark, Dorie. 2013. *Reinventing You: Define Your Brand, Imagine Your Future*. Boston, MA: Harvard Business Review Press.

Coburn, Karen Levin, and Madge Lawrence Treeger. 2009. *Letting Go: A Parents' Guide to Understanding the College Years*. New York: Harper Perennial.

Cohen, Deborah, and Robert Gelfand. 2000. *Just Get Me Through This! A Practical Guide to Coping with Breast Cancer*. New York: Kensington Books.

Cope, Stephen. 2012. *The Great Work of Your Life: A Guide for the Journey to Your True Calling*. Bantam Books Trade Paperback.

Corbett, Rachel. 2016. *You Must Change Your Life: The Story of Rainer Maria Rilke and Auguste Rodin*. New York: W. W. Norton & Co.

Damasio, Antonio. 1999. *The Feeling of What Happens: Body and Emotion in the Making of Consciousness*. New York: Harcourt Brace & Co.

Damour, Lisa. 2017. *Untangled: Guiding Teenage Girls through the Seven Transitions into Adulthood*. New York: Ballantine Books.

Denworth, Lydia. 2020. *Friendship: The Evolution, Biology, and Extraordinary Power of Life's Fundamental Bond*. New York: W. W. Norton & Company.

Dooley, Mike. 2009. *Infinite Possibilities: The Art of Living Your Dreams*. New York: Atria Books.

Dowling, John. 2018. *Understanding the Brain: From Cells to Behavior to Cognition*. New York: W. W. Norton & Company.

Duhigg, Charles. 2019. "The Future of Work: Wealthy, Successful, and Miserable." *New York Times*, February 24, 2019.

Eliot, T. S. 1943. *Four Quartets*.

Farrell, Chris. 2019. *Purpose and a Paycheck: Finding Meaning, Money, and Happiness in the Second Half of Life*. New York: HarperCollins Leadership.

Feiler, Bruce. 2020. *Life Is in the Transitions: Mastering Change at Any Age*. New York: Penguin Press.

Fels, Anna. 2005. *Necessary Dreams: Ambition in Women's Changing Lives*. New York: Anchor Books.

Fisher, Carl Erik. "Calling Addiction a Disease Is Misleading." *New York Times*, January 16, 2022.

Freire, Paulo. 2018. *Pedagogy of the Oppressed*. London: Bloomsbury Academic.

Garcia, Sandra. "After a Tumultuous Year and a Change of Jobs, Ready to Disrupt Again." *New York Times*, October 2, 2018.

Gardner, John W. 1963. *Self-Renewal: The Individual and the Innovative Society*. New York: W. W. Norton & Co.

Gilligan, Carol. 1982. *In a Different Voice: Psychological Theory and Women's Development*. Boston, MA: Harvard University Press.

Gladwell, Malcolm. "The Sure Thing: How Entrepreneurs Really Succeed." *The New Yorker*, January 18, 2010.

Goleman, Daniel. 2004. *Destructive Emotions: A Scientific Dialogue with the Dalai Lama*. New York: Bantam.

Gould, Roger. 1978. *Transformations: Growth and Change in Adult Life*. New York: Simon & Schuster.

Gratton, Lynda, and Andrew Scott. 2020. *The 100-Year Life: Living and Working in an Age of Longevity*. London: Bloomsbury Publishing.

Heller, Caroline. 2015. *Reading Claudius: A Memoir in Two Parts*. New York: The Dial Press/Random House.

Helson, Ravenna M., and Valory Mitchell. 2020. *Women on the River of Life: A Fifty-Year Study of Adult Development*. Berkeley: University of California Press.

Helson, Ravenna, and Geraldine Moane. 1987. "Personality Change in Women from College to Midlife." *Journal of Personality and Social Psychology* 53: 176–86.

Helson, Ravenna, and Sanjay Srivastava. "Three Paths to Adult Development: Conservers, Seekers, and Achievers." *Journal of Personality and Social Psychology* 80, no. 6 (2001): 995–1010.

Helson, Ravenna, and Paul Wink. "Two Conceptions of Maturity Examined in the Findings of a Longitudinal Study." *Journal of Personality and Social Psychology* 53 (1987): 531–41.

Herman, Judith. 2015. *Trauma and Recovery: The Aftermath of Violence from Domestic Abuse to Political Terror*. New York: Basic Books.

Hewlett, Sylvia Ann. 2007. *Off-Ramps and On-Ramps: Keeping Talented Women on the Road to Success*. Boston, MA: Harvard Business School Press.

Hollis, James. 2005. *Finding Meaning in the Second Half of Life: How to Finally Really Grow Up*. New York: Gotham Books.

Holmes, Jamie. 2015. *Nonsense: The Power of Not Knowing*. New York: Crown Publishers.

hooks, bell. 2001. *All About Love: New Visions*. New York: William Morrow.

hooks, bell. 2009. *Belonging: A Culture of Place*. London: Routledge.

hooks, bell. 2004. *Skin Again*. Disney Jump at the Sun.

Horne, Karen. 1945. *Our Inner Conflicts: A Constructive Theory of Neurosis*. W. W. Norton & Company.

Jackson, Richie. 2020. *Gay Like Me: A Father Writes to His Son*. New York: Harper.

Jensen Arnett, Jeffrey. "Conceptions of the Transition to Adulthood: Perspectives from Adolescence Through Midlife." *Journal of Adult Development* 8, no. 2 (2001).

Josselson, Ruthellen. 2017. *Paths to Fulfillment: Women's Search for Meaning and Identity.* Oxford: Oxford University Press.

Josselson, Ruthellen. 1998. *Revising Herself: The Story of Women's Identity from College to Midlife.* Oxford: Oxford University Press.

Judith, Anodea. 2004. *Eastern Body, Western Mind: Psychology and the Chakra System as a Path to the Self.* New York: Celestial Arts/Random House.

Kaufman, Scott. 2020. *Transcend: The New Science of Self-Actualization.* New York: TarcherPerigee.

Keegan, Marina. "Even Artichokes Have Doubts." *Yale Daily News*, September 30, 2011.

Kegan, Robert. 1982. *The Evolving Self: Problem and Process in Human Development.* Boston, MA: Harvard University Press.

Kegan, Robert. 1994. *In Over Our Heads: The Mental Demands of Modern Life.* Boston, MA: Harvard University Press.

Kegan, Robert, and Lisa Laskow Lahey. 2016. *An Everyone Culture: Becoming a Deliberately Developmental Organization.* Boston, MA: Harvard Business Review Press.

Kegan, Robert, and Lisa Laskow Lahey. 2001. *How the Way We Talk Can Change the Way We Work: Seven Languages for Transformation.* New York: Jossey-Bass.

Kegan, Robert, and Lisa Laskow Lahey. 2009. *Immunity to Change: How to Overcome It and Unlock the Potential in Yourself and Your Organization.* Boston, MA: Harvard Business Review Press.

Kidd, Sue Monk. 2016. *The Dance of the Dissident Daughter: A Woman's Journey from Christian Tradition to the Sacred Feminine.* New York: HarperOne.

Lahey, Lisa, Emily Souvaine, Robert Kegan, Robert Goodman, and Sally Felix. 2011. *A Guide to the Subject-Object Interview: Its Administration and Interpretation.* Raymond, NH: Minds at Work.

Lawrence-Lightfoot, Sara. 2012. *Exit: The Endings That Set Us Free.* New York: Sarah Crichton Books.

Lerner, Harriet. 2014. *The Dance of Anger: A Woman's Guide to Changing the Patterns of Intimate Relationships.* New York: William Morrow.

Lerner, Harriet. 1989. *The Dance of Intimacy: A Woman's Guide to Courageous Acts of Change in Key Relationships.* New York: Harper & Row.

Levinson, Daniel, Charlotte Darrow, Edward Klein, Maria Levinson, and Braxton McKee. 1978. *The Seasons of a Man's Life.* New York: Ballantine Books.

Lewchanin, Shari, and Louise Zubrod. "Choices in Life: A Clinical Tool for Facilitating Midlife Review." *Journal of Adult Development* 8, no. 3 (2001).

Lichtwarck-Aschoff, Anna, Paul van Geert, Harke Bosma, and Saskie Kunnen. "Time and Identity: A Framework for Research and Theory Formation." *Developmental Review* 28, no. 3 (2008): 370–400.

"The Lives They Lived." *New York Times Magazine*, December 26, 2021.

Lloyd, Rachel. 2011. *Girls Like Us: Fighting for a World Where Girls Are Not for Sale.* New York: Harper.

McBride, Sarah. 2018. *Tomorrow Will Be Different: Love, Loss, and the Fight for Trans Equality.* New York: Three Rivers Press.

McConnell, Sheri Keys. 2012. *Smart Women Embrace Transitions: How to Lean into Change with Your Body, Mind, and Soul.* New York: Smart Women's Institute, Inc.

"Merging Two Worlds: A Two-Tier Model for Transitioning Youth." *Empower Your Life*, Chapter 1, Lesson 2, Empower Your Future: A Career Readiness Curriculum. GCFGlobal.org. 2003.

Merron, Keith, Dalmar Fisher, and William Torbert. "Meaning Making and Management Action." *Group & Organizational Studies* 12, no. 3 (September 1987).

Miller, Alice, 2007. *The Drama of the Gifted Child: The Search for the True Self.* New York: Basic Books.

Minow, Martha, and Elizabeth Spelman. "In Context." *Southern California Law Review* 63 (1990): 1597–1601.

Mohr, Tara. 2014. *Playing Big: Practical Wisdom for Women Who Want to Speak Up, Create, and Lead.* New York: Avery Penguin Random House.

Mundy, Liza. "Why Is Silicon Valley So Awful to Women?" *The Atlantic*, April 2017.

Napper, Paul, and Anthony Rao. 2019. *The Power of Agency: The 7 Principles to Conquer Obstacles, Make Effective Decisions, and Create a Life on Your Own Terms.* New York: St. Martin's Press.

Norwood, Robin. 1985. *Women Who Love Too Much: When You Keep Wishing and Hoping He'll Change.* New York: Pocket Books/Simon & Schuster.

Ouellette, Jennifer. 2014. *Me, Myself, and Why: Searching for the Science of Self.* New York: Penguin Books.

Pals, Jennifer L. "Narrative Identity Processing of Difficult Life Experiences: Pathways of Personality Development and Positive Self-Transformation in Adulthood." *Journal of Personality* 74 (2006): 1079–1109.

Parker-Pope, Tara. "First, Try to Identify and Name That Emotion." *New York Times*, May 25, 2021.

Peck, M. Scott. 1978. *The Road Less Traveled: A New Psychology of Love, Traditional Values, and Spiritual Growth*. New York: Touchstone.

Peck, M. Scott. 1997. *The Road Less Traveled and Beyond: Spiritual Growth in an Age of Anxiety*. New York: Simon & Schuster, Inc.

Pine, Deborah. "How to Create More Female Business Executives: Start When They're Children." WBUR, April 4, 2017. https://www.wbur.org/cognoscenti/2017/04/04/how-to-create-more-women-business-leaders-deborah-pine.

Pizzolato, Jane Elizabeth. "Assessing Self-Authorship." In *Self-Authorship: Advancing Students' Intellectual Growth: New Directions for Teaching and Learning*, edited by Peggy S. Meszaros, no. 109 (Spring 2007): 31–42.

Richardson, Cheryl. 2017. *Waking Up in Winter*. New York: HarperOne.

Riso, Don Richard, and Russ Hudson. 2000. *Understanding the Enneagram: The Practical Guide to Personality Types*. New York: Houghton Mifflin.

Seligman, Martin. 1990. *Learned Optimism: A Leading Expert on Motivation Demonstrates That Optimism Is Essential for a Good and Successful Life and Shows You How to Acquire It*. New York: Alfred Knopf, Inc.

Sheehy, Gail. 2006. *Passages: Predictable Crises of Adult Life*. New York: Ballantine Books.

Simmons, Rachel. 2018. *Enough as She Is: How to Help Girls Move beyond Impossible Standards of Success to Live Healthy, Happy, and Fulfilling Lives*. New York: HarperCollins.

Sirois, Maria. 2006. *Every Day Counts: Lessons in Love, Faith, and Resilience from Children Facing Illness*. New York: Walker & Co.

Snyder, Rachel Louise. 2019. *No Visible Bruises: What We Don't Know About Domestic Violence Can Kill Us*. London: Bloomsbury Publishing.

Steele, Claude M. 2010. *Whistling Vivaldi: How Stereotypes Affect Us and What We Can Do*. New York: W. W. Norton & Co.

Stewart, Abigail J., Joan M. Ostrove, and Ravenna Helson. "Middle Aging in Women: Patterns of Personality Change from the 30s to the 50s." *Journal of Adult Development* 8 (2001): 23–27.

Talty, Stephan. 2011. *Escape from the Land of Snows: The Young Dalai Lama's Harrowing Flight to Freedom and the Making of a Spiritual Hero*. New York: Crown Random House.

Valliant, George. 2015. *Triumphs of Experience: The Men of the Harvard Grant Study*. Cambridge, MA: Belknap Press.

Van Der Kolk, Bessel. 2015. *The Body Keeps the Score: Brain, Mind, and Body in the Healing of Trauma*. New York: Penguin Books.

Viorst, Judith. 1998. *Necessary Losses: The Loves, Illusions, Dependencies, and Impossible Expectations That All of Us Have to Give Up in Order to Grow.* New York: Simon & Schuster.

White, Elizabeth. 2019. *55, Underemployed, and Faking Normal: Your Guide to a Better Life.* New York: Simon & Schuster.

Book Club Discussion Guide

1. What does the author hope you learn from reading *Dancing with Disruption*?

2. What were your favorite stories in the book? Why did these resonate with you?

3. Which of the author's stories did you like the best? Why?

4. How would you describe this book to a friend?

5. Have you ever encountered a disruption? What about the experience made it disruptive? Recall, a gateway disruption occurs when our experience of the event, feeling, or circumstance *impacts* our ability to function and/or *influences* our thinking about who we are.

6. The author distinguishes between the choices of *change* and *transition* in the wake of a gateway disruption. Have you ever pursued a change or a transition at such a time? Recall, changes leave intact our beliefs about who we are, and transitions invite us to re-examine the assumptions upon which we architect our sense of self.

7. Have you ever grown? What was it like to undertake such a journey? Recall, transformative growth is a process of coming into our own voices.

8. The author introduces the Incubator, a toolkit to support our personal transformation. What was your favorite part of the Incubator? Why? Recall, the Incubator includes Reframing Emotions, Resetting Expectations, Reimagining Identity, and Reconstituting Connections.

9. Imagine you are asked to summarize *Dancing with Disruption* for a person who has just experienced a life-altering disruption. What would you say?

10. What do you hope you will remember from this book the next time you experience a disruption?

Index

Page references for figures are italicized.

About the Author

Linda Rossetti is a pioneering writer, researcher, and business leader who is committed to advancing our understanding of transformation and growth in adult lives.

A leading authority on identity renewal, her research has been featured on NPR, NECN/NBC, *Money* magazine, Next Avenue, and other outlets. She hosts the podcast *Destination Unknown: A Field Guide* and is the founder of The Transition Institute, LLC, whose mission is to advance the research and practice of individual and organizational transformation. Her first book, *Women and Transition: Reinventing Work and Life*, offers a new perspective on the benefits of growth in one's personal and professional life.

Linda has worked at the intersection of growth and transformation throughout her professional career. As executive vice president of human resources and administration at Iron Mountain, she helped transform the business into a digital records management leader by combining more than two hundred acquisitions into one organization. As CEO of eMaven, Inc., a venture capital–backed technology company, she led the digital transformation of some of the largest companies in the United States. Her extensive not-for-profit and for-profit board service has supported many organizations in their strategic evolution and growth.

Linda holds an MBA from Harvard and a bachelor's degree in economics from Simmons University. She is the proud parent of two teenagers and a goldendoodle named Apollo. Learn more at https://lindarossetti.com/.

CONTINUE THE CONVERSATION!

I would love to continue the conversation with you at LindaRossetti.com. There, you can contact me and gain access to additional resources to support your journey. Please keep in mind that my last name is spelled with two *s*'s and two *t*'s—a tricky one!

Please follow me on social media. I look forward to talking with you!

Instagram: @LindaRossettiAuthor

Facebook: @LindaRossettiAuthor

LinkedIn: https://www.linkedin.com/in/lindarossetti/

Subscribe to my podcast: *Destination Unknown: A Field Guide*

9 781538 169377